Leaf Lessons

Leaf Lessons

When Trauma & Religion Collide

The Process of Spiritual Awakening & Healing.

Author Angie Harris

Edited by: Clelia Lewis

Cover art by: logolrux

Photographs: The Wait

Dedication & Acknowledgements

There are so many I want to thank for supporting me on this journey of healing—those who inspired me during the completion of this book and those who walked alongside me. At times I find myself in awe of how the Divine lines up our lives so that we are where we are meant to be at the right time, right place, and with the right people. I suppose I should not be surprised that things aligned this way even in the completion of this book. Yet still, I get goosebumps thinking about how this book was guided by something much higher than myself.

I dedicate this book to my dad. I give thanks for my dad's support in this creation. Though he is not here physically, I felt him pushing and encouraging me throughout this process. Had I not begun to feel his presence I am unsure if this book would have been developed in the way it was. I miss you being here dad, but I'm grateful for your guidance on this journey, even as you are enjoying all the bliss of the other side.

My editor. I was worried about finding someone who would be aligned with this book and the sensitive nature of the subject matter. I truly believe I was led to someone who could hold my story and help it come to life. Not only did you align with my story, you became an extension of it. Clelia, you are amazing, and I could not have asked for someone more perfect to edit my first book. Thank you for your wisdom, insight, and clarity in helping bring this work to life. My best friend, Lin! A you are a soul mate and sister. A woman who has seen me go through it all. I love you. Thank you for blessing me by your continued support. Thank you for being secure enough in yourself to hold space for both my flaws and my success. Your continued support and love as I navigate through this life is a blessing. Our "Oprah & Gail" friendship is one I deeply cherish. You inspire me and make my life more beautiful.

Joette, I was on a mission to find deep healing, unsure where it would be found. There is no other way to describe the process of finding you other than divine guidance. Your support on my healing journey has been pivotal and life transforming. Being fully authentic, and genuinely caring, you have always held space for me, seen me, believed me, and continue to teach me how to live my life in alignment with my highest self. You inspire me by your own healing and courageous journey to move forward. Those who have the privilege to work with you and know you are truly blessed. Thank you for being a guiding light and providing the safety to "make myself at home," exposing my bare feet and heart. Your presence in my life is a huge part of why this book exists.

Dr. Diane McMillen, I think back to the days spent in your classroom in college and how much knowledge I gained. I was so resistant to the teachings back then, but they have since become a source of healing and inspiration for me to live out my life boldly and freely, diving into my calling as a healer. You inspire me, and everyone who knows you. This world is truly better because you spent this lifetime doing what you were called to do.

Lastly, to all the friends cheering for me and supporting me—all of those who walked alongside me in the years prior to this book being created, and those who continue to—thank you for being in my life. I am thankful for the love you provided me and continue to.

I am truly blessed.

Love, Angie

Contents

Poem

Sacred Sanctuary

Find yourself amongst the trees

the wildflowers, streams, and breeze

where none may find you but the light through the
leaves

and your spirit awaken, simple and free.

Preface

I hope you find love in these pages. I hope you enjoy the journey with me. I invite you to cry, laugh, think, wonder, and be challenged. If you want to get angry, get angry. If you want to question me, question me. If you don't agree, then don't! I don't expect your journey to be my journey. We each have a unique path suited to us with its own obstacles and challenges, and we each have unique strengths and things we need to learn to navigate. If we were all the same there would be nothing new to learn. If we did not have any darkness in the world, we would never know the beauty of the light. If we did not experience loss, we would not know what it felt like to love something or someone so much we grieved. If we did not have hurt or disagreement, there would be no need for forgiveness or for finding ways to reconcile with others—both of which bring about the most profound experience of love there is to find. So many things we see as negative are the universe's way of pushing us toward positive growth. I don't want to dismiss that there are VERY hard things we go through. Trust me, you will find some of that in this book. I have deep seated trauma—I know what that is. But I know what healing is too. If I can work through my own trauma toward healing, I know anyone can. That is my wish for you. These are the Leaf Lessons: learning to let go of control and let the flow of universal love hold you in its embrace.

Worthy of Healing

The things you read in this book are not written with the purpose of provoking, persuading, or changing your beliefs, views, outlook on things you may believe, or how you see the world. The words you read in this book are my real experiences of trauma, overcoming trauma, and how I have come to understand the world through my own personal spiritual awakening. I believe we each have our own soul's purpose, and this is the story of how I found mine. I do hope, however, that these words inspire you and help you to find your own healing, maybe even help you in your spiritual awakening if you are seeking it. I hope that through the journey of reading these pages you are inspired to search for your soul's purpose, the reason you came to this earth. My desire is that you are inspired to heal, grow, learn, and become who you were created to be, the person the world needs you to be. I truly believe deep inside each one of us is someone great just waiting to come out.

I come humbly before you, knowing that I do not have all the answers in life, only my experiences and understanding of what I have grown through and the many lessons I have had on my journey. You may not agree with many of the things I mention throughout these pages, and that is okay. We are all different, and that is important. If we were all the same, the world would be a very boring place. So please, read with an open mind and lens. I write from a place of compassion, love, and a genuine heart, as well as from an understanding of trauma, both my own and that of the many souls I have been privileged to help. Some readers may only have a peripheral understanding of the types of experiences I share in this book, while others may understand from the depths of their own personal experience and pain. To those, I send you my love as you work through your own process, and I caution you to stop reading if anything triggers you. Take space and treat yourself with compassion, allow yourself to be in the moment without need to change or feel shame for whatever feelings arise. Give yourself grace to be who you are without judgment. Know that you are in the right place in your journey no matter what, and trust your instincts about whether this book is a healing influence for you in this current moment or season. I do believe if you picked this book up and are reading it, there is likely a reason. I invite you to keep an open mind. Perhaps by the end of it you will find direction in your healing journey or spiritual awakening. If not, maybe there is a different kind of lesson within these pages for you, and somewhere down the road you will understand what it is, remembering the words you read.

It is not my desire to change you, only challenge you. It is a challenge myself to write the words of this book and to share my story, to open up about things I have not before and to share the few details of my awakening with the world. I am aware of how it causes triggers as I myself felt them in the process of recording the stories on these pages. But whether you are uncomfortable because you are reminded of something you experienced in your life, or because you become upset or angry, or simply because you disagree and it is rubbing against a concept you believe in or challenging your worldview, please keep in mind that triggers are not always bad, they just show us something that we need to pay attention to.

I've been attempting to write this book for at least ten years in fits and starts. I would write freely for three or four chapters and then get stuck each time. I never understood why until now. Back then, the book was about being a single Christian woman in the church. I was a devoted Christian at the time, trying to remain celibate and "pure" so I could be ready for my future husband, "good enough" for him, pure enough, not completely "used up." I had this bright idea about interviewing all the single women in the church about their lives, young and old, how they had been able to remain celibate all their lives, or if they weren't able to, what their challenges were. "Tell me, how do you not have sex?" I think back to that time and giggle to myself at how committed I was to the mission of helping singles in the church abstain from sex.

Side note: If you have any desire to perform one of these interviews, please share it with me. I am very curious about your discovery! I guarantee you will find many singles who have struggled their entire lives with "impure thoughts" and feeling "bad" for having "lustful desires" in any way. Most likely, they will have struggled with some form of sexual "acting out," if they aren't actually having sex.

I remember sitting in church week after week thinking about how none of the services were useful to me in my struggles with being single. There was no guidance for how to live without a partner and accept celibacy. Occasionally, someone would bring up a verse about being blessed to be single and how it is a "calling." I remember thinking, *God, I don't want to be blessed! I don't want that calling! Where is my man! I need sex!* I was so messed up by the religious talk and this unattainable expectation that I would be completely pure by sheer force of will, "fully relying on god" (my 90's friends will know this one: FROG), holding back this terrible beast of sexual desire. I truly believed if I didn't contain it, I wouldn't get the relationship I wanted, and I would possibly go to hell because I wasn't really following Jesus.

Those in the church would say, "Jesus loves you, and if you accept Him as your savior, you are saved and will go to Heaven." And then again, "But, you will be judged harshly and are at risk of not really being saved, so you better repent if you think anything bad or have any lustful thoughts." It was a mess of, "Yes, no, and, but, maybe, just in case, you better be careful, do what is right because the judgment and the risk and the what ifs, and the consequences are real." I can't tell you the years I spent in torment, believing I was "bad," how many alter calls I did trying to make myself pure, hoping to take all of my horrible, impure thoughts away, trying to NOT think about anything sexual towards a man or woman again. I had NO idea that because of the things I had been through in my life, I also was struggling with a brain and nervous system full of trauma and the truth was that no willpower, no matter how hard I tried, was going to change it. Because of my trauma from years of abuse and the negative programming of my mind, there was no way I was going to make it just disappear. But I tried. I tried as hard as I could. I wrote down my prayers every night, *Please God, take these desires away from me. Help me not have any impure thoughts. Help me be completely pure so I can one day get a husband and be good enough for you.*

Each time I told myself I wasn't good enough because of my "sin" or struggles, each time I was told I was bad because of them, I internalized these beliefs and drove them down onto the earlier traumas, compounding them further. I was filled with negative thinking, turning to more and more performance-based behaviors for the church, and even people outside of the church, to prove my worth. It wasn't until I was close to thirty-eight years old that I would find myself breaking free from this thinking—it has been a long, slow process, which I continue to work on.

Things in my life have taken a complete turn in the past seven years. Not only has my mission in life changed, but I no longer believe in abstaining from sex outside of marriage. I don't go to church, or relate in the same way to the religious teachings I learned there. I do consider myself to be spiritual, but religion is no longer a part of who I am. I know this book will find many other "book friends" on the shelves, as I have spent the last few years reading other books, listening to podcasts and YouTube channels, and visiting with friends and people who have been placed in my life who, like me, have gone through changes in thinking towards their spiritual journey. My beliefs and understanding of the world have changed drastically, my thinking and way of being in life have as well, and this book became something completely different from my original idea.

I have come to understand that the block in completing my personal life story was a divine intervention of God. God stopped me from writing the book because it was not meant to be written in that context. Sometimes we are divinely redirected from things we are not meant to do, and don't understand why until later. I became frustrated with myself for not being able to complete the book, thinking I would never get it done, and wondering if my instinct to write it in the first place was mistaken. Now I know the instinct was real, and beginning to write opened the door to this book, the one meant to be written.

A few people who know me personally may experience a shock as they read the words in this book, not knowing that this transition has happened in my life. Some may know a little about the trauma I have experienced but be surprised to know how much I kept hidden all of my life. Others will read it, unsurprised by most of it, but shocked by the spiritual awakening process, knowing they had watched something happen in me, but unaware what it was. There may be others that will think I've left my belief in God, have gone to the "dark side," and am walking down a trail straight to hell. Yet others who have walked alongside me for some of my journey will be inspired, as I have been inspired by them. However, my main reason for writing it is to help those who desire healing, who may be in the process of being awakened, possibly working through much of their own trauma personally and religiously, and to let them know they are not alone. My hope is to help inspire those on this journey to push forward when it is hard, and to believe in themselves and the power within them to manifest their true self and dreams; to find their divine belonging and being within themselves and the world; to learn to love themselves; to look in the mirror and, perhaps for the first time, to like what they see; to begin to seek their inner consciousness and connect with this part of themselves more than they do the past trauma or their ego; to move from a mindset of fear to a mindset of freedom.

I admit, it can be a lonely journey at times, and there is no exact formula for how to do it. It is a step by step, day by day process of slowly letting go of your grip on the familiar and embracing the unknown. But I do know that it is important to allow those who are divinely placed in your path to support you and hold you up when you are wanting to give up or are unsure whether you are losing your mind or tapping into something amazing. And if you don't give up, if you keep pushing through, eventually, through this very slow process, you evolve. You may not even see it happening. Before you know it, you look at yourself in the mirror, or you talk to a friend, or you engage in an activity and you see yourself differently. You notice you react differently. You start liking things you didn't like before, not wanting to do things you enjoyed doing before, and walking away from things you never thought you'd walk away from. You might have friends who suddenly disappear, or you just feel different around them or can't relate to them any longer. You'd rather spend time at home meditating and reading or studying a skill, or in nature connecting with Mother Earth's energy, than at a party or shopping with friends. You still enjoy those things, but it is no longer your first priority. You just know that there is more to life. You desire more and you know it requires a deeper healing, not just on a surface level, but spiritually.

I'm not sure how else to explain it other than one day you look back and think, "How did I get here?" You may even look at pictures of yourself from a few months ago, a year ago, or two years ago, or even five years ago, and not recognize that person anymore. I have had that experience several times. At times I look at the person I was and wonder what she was thinking, what did she feel, how sad she looked. I feel sad for her even now, how much hurt she held in her body, how much sadness she felt the need to hide inside her in fear of what people would think of her if she exposed it. She had no idea that exposing it was the very thing that would free her; that releasing the trauma from her body was what would give her the freedom to walk out of her shell and no longer fear herself; that she would be able to sit with a group of friends and not care if they were judging her, talking about her behind her back, or if she fit in with them—it didn't matter because she knew she was worthy just as she was.

She had no inkling then that she would discover herself to be a being of light and energy; that once she opened up and spoke her truth, the years of hurt, pain, suicidal thoughts, anger, sadness, fear, terror, abuse, abandonment, all of it, would heal mentally and physically; that she would lose the weight she was working so hard to lose without spending countless, pointless hours working out with no result, that it would no longer seem to be the biggest priority of her day, and she would become more relaxed in who she was.

She had no idea, after years of searching for solutions to her endometriosis only to end up having a hysterectomy at age thirty-six, no longer able to bear children, that she would be able to heal and understand why she went through the experience; that she would be able to accept herself and understand that it was not her fault. She was not aware of the trauma that caused her body to work against her for so many years.

She did not know that the many years she spent holding herself back and not believing in her own potential was because she believed she was bad, nor that holding the traumas inside was only compounding her pain, nor that the unprocessed emotions, feelings, and negative beliefs about being a sinner needing to be saved or be damned to hell was causing her to strive to become something other than herself, to live up to a standard that she would never be able to reach.

She did not know it was only when she finally let all this go, she would finally be able to live; that then, for the first time in her life learning boundaries, embracing her own voice, being able to say no, and accepting help from others, she would begin to love herself and through loving herself, she would grow, and this growth would bring something she never expected—a woman, a being of light and love with purpose and the ability to serve others as she had always wanted.

Trauma, Religion, and Awakening

I had no idea how much was inside me: the mental and emotional anguish, the pain in my body, the anger. I had no clue what I was holding for so long. I felt devoid of hope, a lost cause. My life was one constant cycle of chaos followed by digging out of it to achieve a fleeting moment of liberation only to freeze in fear, unable to move forward, my hopes and dreams falling away once again. I felt compelled to stay small and insignificant in the world. I would get a glimpse of my future once in a while, in dreams, or visions, knowing there was more for me on the other side of all my fear, but I blamed myself for not having the strength to push through. Once in a while I would share these visions and dreams with others only to feel ignored, shut down, or condescendingly assured that one day I might speak about something on a stage. No one else believed in me so why should I? I didn't know how to get past the blocks that were keeping me paralyzed in fear. So I learned to keep silent.

My own silence further paralyzed me. I had convinced myself that I felt safe in it. It was my shelter. What was on the other side wasn't safe. Speaking out seemed simple in my head, but when it came to actually doing it, I felt as if something or someone was holding my throat shut. I feared exposing what I held inside, that anyone who heard or saw it would judge me and lower their view of me. Not that I thought anyone's beliefs or view of me was very high in the first place, but I didn't want them any lower. I hoped that if I just worked hard and became good at a few things without showing my scars, maybe they wouldn't be seen—but they always seemed to reveal themselves in some way and shame would take over and I would retreat. At times I was so fearful of my scars being shown I couldn't return to the place they were exposed. I knew I was safe if I stayed hidden, and maybe the scars and my silence where my true friends.

Possibly I believed that the scars were what helped seal all the pain inside me so I didn't have to bleed anymore. Even though the scar tissue was painful in its own way, it felt better than having to dig at and expose the pain inside. I didn't like to feel the pain inside my body—why would anyone else want to feel it, see my scars, or hear about them? I never told anyone about what caused the scars. If they did see them, I would just make a joke about it, or a small story about it, then we would move on, and I would just pretend it didn't bother me. Why tell the story after all these years? I was fine, I was always fine. I had made it this long. I had fully convinced myself.

Even so, I let the pain out in the silence of my own hidden spaces and in small doses to others— never to anyone who could be there all the time, nor see it full on. If I revealed too much I panicked. I didn't trust they would stay and, of course, they didn't, either because I left or because they became uncomfortable and left me. Knowing what I know now, it is likely that I sabotaged the relationships of my own accord in some way in order to stay hidden.

At the age of eighteen I sat on my bed feeling numb and defeated, drinking some sort of alcohol (as I always did when I felt upset) and taking a bottle of pills. It wasn't my first attempt at suicide, but it was my first serious one. That night I actually prayed to "Satan" to take my life. I told God that if he didn't want to kill me, I knew Satan did. I went to sleep that night after drinking the alcohol and taking the bottle of pills, fully believing I would die. Disappointed the next morning when I woke up, I remember feeling angry and confused. But at the same time, something inside me had the thought, *Maybe I am here for a purpose*. It was then I decided I had to find a way to figure it out.

I knew I was made to help people. I always had that desire in me. Of course I didn't realize that to help others I needed to heal myself. It wasn't until years later when I jumped into the healing and mental health field that I began my own healing journey. My career in this field lasted for fifteen years. I am grateful that during that time I was able to help others, if in a limited way. But I know it was when I began to heal myself that my true capacities began to emerge. Once I came to the realization that I had my own trauma to heal, and as painful as it might be I must do it to reveal who I was truly meant to be, I began the journey of digging down into the mud, into the reality, and speaking it out of my body.

When I began my healing journey, I realized that the scars formed around my trauma had not actually protected me or healed me, but rather had left the tissue beneath inflamed and festering due to ignoring the underlying wounds, keeping silent for so long, and stuffing pain down inside my body. I needed "surgery" to open myself back up if I were to do any kind of reconstruction—all those traumas had to be seen and exposed. I knew this but I tried to avoid it for many years. It meant remembering how it felt and possibly the actual experiences too. I have had a lot of experiences in my body. At times it felt as if there might be too many things to work through, that I was a lost cause and might as well give up on my healing and just remain as I was. Yet at the same time I had an intuition that I was someone who could provide a beneficial impact in the world. Somehow, something in me kept pushing me forward, blindly.

Then I experienced a series of events that started to point me in the direction I needed to take to begin this "surgery," the process of digging into my deep-seated traumas and memories of the past held within my subconscious. There was so much hidden there because I had dissociated myself from the pain in order to survive. Now I began to run smack into the face of my trauma as I ran into several people I had not seen in over twenty years, began remembering things from my childhood, and started having dreams about events from my past. There was no denying something was pushing me to start the process of healing. I did not know what was happening, but my life was starting to shift in ways I could not explain and I began to have an uneasy feeling about everything.

What I can say about this process (which I call my awakening) is that it required complete vulnerability. This kind of healing is not an easy road to take. As I said before, it can be lonely, you can feel isolated and set apart. You may find yourself detaching from friends, family, things you once enjoyed, or even no longer wanting to participate in activities you always did. Your habits may change, you may find yourself exploring things you once thought to be evil, you may find yourself doing things you thought you would never do, things that scared you because you feared what they would bring into your life. One of the things that happened to me in my awakening was I lost the desire to overindulge in alcohol. As a Christian, I justified my drinking by saying, "Jesus turned water into wine, so it is fine!" I drank to cover up my unresolved pain. I drank to numb myself to who I was so I could show up as a person I was not. As I opened myself more and more, allowing the painful feelings I had been avoiding, and as I learned to love myself for who I actually am, the need to drink to cover up or numb myself fell away. Now I may have a drink occasionally, but I no longer have that desire to indulge like I did.

I also no longer have the desire to fit into society as I once did. A lot of the behaviors I engaged in then were an attempt to fit into the world. Because I often felt so separated from the world, the only way I knew how to fit into it was by doing the things I saw others do, even if they were destructive to me. I started going to church in my teens, doing whatever I needed to do to fit in there. At the same time, I was hiding away from experiences at home. I found myself caught between my new identity as a believer and my old identity as the person I was outside of the church. When I wanted to connect with someone outside of the church, I would shift my behavior to conform to those people, and when I was in the church, I shifted my behavior back to be a good follower of Jesus.

Without knowing it, I was losing my own identity more and more as I tried to become something I was not, desperately hoping to find a way to fit in somewhere. I really had no idea who I was or what I wanted in life. I was lost, sad, hurting, and just searching for love and acceptance.

In my awakening, drinking is just one example of desires that fell away. You may find that you have different areas of your life that you no longer want to engage in if you have had a similar experience. For me, I had no idea who I was. I would speak about being a Christian and having my identity "in Christ," but I had no idea what that meant. The words I read on the pages of the bible didn't go into my heart, transform my spirit, or cause me to become awakened to my true divine being that was created to be good and loving on this earth. It wasn't because I wasn't trying—I was trying with everything in me. I would read the words of Jesus about "Love your neighbor and love one another" and always showed up as someone who put others first. But in the middle of putting others first, I lost myself. No one ever took the time to tell me (or at least I didn't experience it) that it is in loving yourself that you learn how to love others.

In my awakening, I have moved away from believing the bible is the divinely spoken word of God, to understanding it as a religious book created over many years by men to reflect their own beliefs about God and spirit and society. I do believe that some of the writings in it are words spoken to people that heard from God, or were written by those who may have been around Jesus or known someone who knew Jesus or heard about a teaching Jesus taught. But I had been told that it was the very word of God spoken and written down directly from God with no flaw in it at all, and I believed it for a long time. It is no longer a belief I hold on to. I have done much study in this area and have discovered that most of the New Testament was written much later after Jesus died and that the Old Testament was written by numerous individuals at different times, and all of these combined books were combed through and many were added to or rejected by church patriarchs hundreds of years later, leaving only those things that confirmed or supported their own world-view. The truth is that men decided they had God's permission to change the bible because it wasn't depicting who they wanted God to be. Then they added verses about not adding anything to the bible—but only after what they added!

I have come to understand in my awakening that God still talks to us today and that prophecy and divine words are still being spoken today. If we still felt allowed to add to the bible, it would likely be continually added to, rewritten, or tossed out altogether and a new one created, maybe even with more truth, light, and love in it.

I personally believe that in an effort to control women, men began to rewrite and manipulate the bible in a way that would justify their domination over others, especially women, and convince women of their inferiority and their need to follow and obey men. (As most Christians know, the bible teaches that wives must obey their husbands. I don't say any of this to demean Christians or their beliefs. I think there is a time for roles and for masculine energy and feminine energies to be shared in a relationship. However, when it comes to one controlling the other, I do not agree.) I found this attitude to be very present in how the church I attended taught purity, especially when it came to the role of sex between a man and a woman.

Of course, both men and women are expected by the church to "save" themselves for marriage, but the bulk of the burden is on the women's and girls' shoulders. It is the women and girls who must be responsible for how they present themselves; emphasis is placed on their job of shielding their "brothers" from sinning, while not much is placed on the men to keep their eyes from wandering or learn to manage their urges. Looking at how much sexual abuse has happened within the walls of many churches, it should come as no surprise that the men of the church have become predators of children and women. The men are taught to neglect their God-given desires for the sake of serving a god that gave those same desires to them, and then without fail, they are unable to control them. I do think there are some men who are able to manage their desires and I applaud them! However, for naturally sexual beings, pure suppression is likely to backfire.

Ironically, the church often teaches that Jesus came to abolish the law while also teaching that homosexuality is wrong, that one must obey god and sacrifice oneself for the sake of being loved, that women must obey their husbands, and so on—as if Jesus' death did not really count for certain individuals, only those who are living a life aligned with the current "laws" of the church.

One of the first things I learned upon entering the church was that I needed to get rid of all of my non-Christian music because it would take me off my path to obeying god and living a life that is pure. I went on "purity retreats" at which I was told that I shouldn't wear certain clothing items, say certain words, hang out with non-believers or participate in activities with them (unless I was there to witness and help them find god). I was told to have a daily quiet time, read my bible, and pray. I had constant guilt over a missed day of reading my bible or praying. I also felt horrible that I preferred hanging out with my non-Christian friends more than my Christian friends.

In my awakening I have come to understand that some of these "rules" and guidelines I learned in the church could be useful, but the way they were presented was not always in a life-positive way. Rather than suggested as tools for creating peace of mind or contacting inner guidance, they were presented as absolutes to be obeyed or risk being damned to hell, rejected by god and not loved for who I was. Once more, on top of the trauma in my body, I believed I had to change who I was to be accepted, to be safe. However, that is not really the case. That is not required by God. God actually wants us to become who we authentically are, not try to be something or someone we are not.

Now I understand how useful it can be to keep my mind pure and of my own free will I choose to do so in certain ways. But that is only because I have come to understand that things such as anxiety, perfectionism, and some ideas that I have developed over my life do not align with my spirit and true self. They cause me to not love myself and that is not what God wants. God wants us to love ourselves, and to love ourselves we must make decisions that align with our highest good, and sometimes that means giving up things that might be preventing our healing or that block our potential behind unhealed trauma.

I always knew I wanted to do something in my life to help people and I believed that I would find my calling within the church setting, which led me to a Christian college where I found myself in the same scenarios as before—wandering off campus to the "secular" university to hang out with non-Christians. I received repeated warnings that if I did not straighten up my act, I was at risk of being kicked out of the school. During my freshman year I was even kicked out of the dorm suite I was living in for getting in a fight with my roommate that almost turned physical. I can't remember exactly what we got in a fight about, but it must have been significant enough that the school felt I needed to be moved to a completely different floor of the dorm with all new girls. I didn't feel like I fit in with the new girls at all and had a hard time the rest of the year.

It was at this college I met my best friend, who still remains in this role even today, an Indigenous Native American who I will call Lin. Lin and I hung out all the time those first two semesters before I was moved to a different suite for not getting along with my roommate, but once I was moved, we began to struggle in our friendship. Over the years we had our ups and downs, mostly due to my behaviors and struggles from unresolved trauma. I remember I shared some stories with her about my life in that first year of college, but not a lot. At eighteen and nineteen years of age, neither of us really knew much about life, though we thought we did. We came from very different backgrounds. Hers was a strong Christian family home, while mine was unstable, divorced, non-Christian, and carried a lot of trauma. I had a hard time relating to some of her views on life and she mine. We both have strong personalities and neither of us are afraid to speak our minds. In a way, this brought us together but it also caused us to disagree a lot as well.

One day as we were fighting about something, I became angry with her for acting as if she was better than me and more advanced in her walk with God. I looked her in the eyes and said, "Okay, Ms. MOST-Perfect-Christian-in-the-World!" We were both stunned. Suddenly we saw we were not in the same place in our faith. We took a long break from our friendship after that. We both remember it vividly and laugh about it now, but it was a pivotal moment in each of our lives. I realized I did not want to be like the many Christians I saw around me —arrogant and holding myself above others—while she realized the potential harm of her faith causing pride. She left the college after that year. I continued for two more before I left. It has been interesting to revisit that conversation now as adults who have been through many changes. We are both in a similar place with our understanding of God and we both look back on that moment as humorous yet significant in our friendship and in our individual journeys.

It shows both of us how religion can cause people to separate and divide, how it can be used against others, even justifying unloving behavior. If you look at most of the religions in the world, splits and disagreements, even violence is common on many levels. Our small dispute was just one example of how something can be twisted and used to break people apart, how people can become entrenched in dogmatic beliefs, developing completely different understandings about what they presume to be the same thing—God.

I say all this to help you understand that I write this book from a very strong religious background. I became a Christian at the age of 16, went to bible college, did missionary work in India, Laos, Thailand, Los Angeles, and Chicago. I taught bible studies, led youth groups, led purity retreats for youth, studied the bible front to back, memorizing names and places, highlighting and taking notes on every verse, studying and comparing the different versions of the bible. I did it all. I wanted to know it all—to be educated in the bible in all areas so I could be who I was supposed to be in the world. Everything I write in these pages comes from a place of deep understanding of the conventional Christian path to which I was thoroughly committed.

From an early age I felt different from others, an outsider who didn't fit in, even with friends and family. I never had a place I felt I belonged. It felt as if I was just traveling through life, waiting for something to happen, for something inside me to be exposed and discovered and one day come out. I didn't know what it was but I wanted to find it. I spent years seeking it in the bible, in a relationship to what I thought was God. I didn't find it there, but the process of seeking itself slowly began to uncover this inner part of me, eventually manifesting my awakening.

When I awoke, I realized that knowing you are different and embracing that uniqueness allows you to start to enhance your gifts and vibrate at a higher frequency. When you start to enhance your frequency, some things fall away while other new things attract you. It is called the law of attraction, which I am sure many of you reading this have heard of. When you walk at a higher frequency, you can't help but attract new experiences and situations. This went against everything I learned in the church and was a hard thing to embrace. In the church I was told that such ideas were demonic and to stay away from them. I was fearful of anything that would allow demonic forces or darkness into my life as I had had many experiences of coming face to face with dark spirits—or so I believed. In my awakening, however, I have come to understand these experiences differently and have learned to love manifesting things in my life. This book is one of those things I am manifesting. And in the process of writing this book, I have already started to work on a second book that came to me in a dream.

Seven years ago, I could not have imagined sitting here writing a book about how my views have changed from rigid, religion-based, trauma-based thinking, to spirit centered thinking that includes an understanding of energy, meditation, chakras, and speaking to spirits. I could not have imagined working on healing past traumas because I had no idea I needed to heal, or that I needed to be freed from negative beliefs. I didn't know that I was not fully loving myself, accepting myself, or working towards my highest good.

Even a year ago I would not have imagined writing this book. The darkness that covered my thinking kept me in such a blocked energy that I was unable to see any light. Thinking back to the original title I was going to give this book, "Living Single in a Couples World," I can't imagine publishing something like that now. However, IF I did, it would be full of encouragement and freedom! Telling people to embrace their single life, or even become single if they are in a marriage that is damaging to their self-worth or no longer serving their higher good. I'm not even sure I believe in marriage anymore. A contract saying "I am yours forever" is not something I am interested in. A partner, yes, but a contract, no. I am more interested in finding someone I would feel free to be myself with; someone I could let see my soul; someone spiritually committed to growing with me in this life, if it is serving my higher good; someone to radiate at the same frequency as myself, to live at a high vibration of love and light, and to manifest that out into the world with me, working towards the betterment of not just ourselves, but the world around us. I do not feel the need to place a label on whether that person is a male or female. I believe a soul mate can come in any physical form. It is the spirit that matters. I also believe that the spiritual bond is the most powerful bond. I have come to understand that the spirit is not a sex—as God is not a sex.

I have learned many lessons in my search for the truth, deconstructing old beliefs, leaving religion, rebuilding my sense of self-worth, and healing. I am still in the process—I believe we are all constantly growing. To believe one has arrived at the destination is to become prideful or stagnant or even narcissistic. No longer believing you have anything to work on means no longer truly living. We all have a purpose on this earth. All of us are here to find our higher selves, our light and energy we are to manifest. To find our soul's purpose and give it to the world. Whether we find it in this lifetime or next doesn't matter. Maybe in my next lifetime I will come back and read this book, and it will help me remember I am on a spiritual journey to find my true self, to learn about love and how I can spread it among others. Of course, I hope to achieve that in this lifetime before I leave this earth, and live it to the fullest, manifesting my potential and helping others to do so as well. I fully believe we all have something special deep inside of us just waiting to be discovered.

The Show Must Go On

Life often comes in cycles. Those cycles are life lessons. Have you ever noticed that just when it seems you've made it through a difficult challenge, mastered that level so you can finally relax, all of a sudden something else pops up? Usually it is completely different but has a familiar feeling to it. It can seem as if life always has an obstacle in the way, a mountain to climb, or a barrier to get to the next level.

From an early age, I faced challenges. My parent's divorced when I was small, I struggled to make friends in school, I was bullied in elementary school, overweight, depressed, anxious, carried physical pain, emotional pain, experienced sexual abuse and mental abuse. My mom did her best and was around most of the time, but she wasn't very emotionally available due to her own trauma. My dad was even less present, his own dad not having been around for him growing up.

Family cycles—from the inside they are virtually impossible to see, and even harder to speak about. But often, there will be one person in a family that sees the patterns, feels them most intensely, and manifests the pain of them outwardly. They can often be the one to break the silence and potentially the generational cycle. I have been in this position in relation to my family of origin. However, I do not have my own children, which raises the question: How might I be able to help heal a family cycle that I am not going to physically contribute to in the form of bearing children?

I have had the privilege of many kids in my life— mentoring them, working with them in the mental health field, and as a foster parent for a short time. I adore kids and have cherished and loved some of them as my own, teaching them their worth and how to love themselves. Working in the mental health field, I tried to give them a glimpse of love, healing, and a hope for becoming healthy, whole adults one day. I am sure I was not always successful, but I tried. There are a few of them I've stayed in touch with who are now adults—they are beautiful, successful humans. I still encourage and mentor them and enjoy every moment I get to have with them. I am thankful for these relationships. But I still wonder how to bring healing to my own family.

I am not the first in my family to not have children. My granny, who I spent much time with as I was growing up, never had children of her own. She was not my biological grandmother, of course, but she played a significant role in our lives—for myself, my brother, and for my mother. She helped to raise us, and was present in a way my parents couldn't be. Maybe her presence was even a part of breaking some of our cycles.

You may notice yourself struggling with many of the same things your parents struggled with, and their parents struggled with. Patterns of behavior, addictions, emotional postures, ways of thinking can be passed down for generations. It takes tremendous awareness of oneself to see such patterns and choose to break free of them. It is not easy to be that person in the family who sees and wants to break out of the cycle. Family structures are familiar and have functioned to create a stability (even if a dysfunctional one) that does not give way easily to change. To be an agent of change can cause one to feel like an outcast, facing the obstacles no one else sees.

This has been my calling, though I didn't realize it until recently. I decided it was time to deal with my shit—like really deal with it. I often felt odd—in all settings, even with my own family. Even as a small child, I stood out, I was different, and I knew I was. I had odd experiences that others didn't. I "saw" things that "weren't there," I felt things, and I always had a sense that there was something else to this thing called life. I had a hard time making friends, I didn't fit in the circles with other girls my age, and I struggled in school. It always seemed as if I had this intense energy in a room that drew attention in a negative way. I could sense I had a strength, that I could walk in a room and the whole room's energy shifted. I never knew why. I didn't necessarily like it, and I just wanted to be "normal."

But I realized over the last few years that I was set apart from birth for a purpose. I am a healer, and my energy is different because of this. My experiences in life caused me to forget who I was and become silent, fearful, and to try to fit into the world, cramming myself into shoes that didn't fit. I worked to become the strong person I had to be to make it in life. I didn't want to be seen as weak, so instead of being an empathic healer, I became a strong, silent warrior. My silence became my armor. I am reminded of a song by Freddie Mercury of Queen, called "The Show Must Go On."

Empty spaces, what are we living for?
Abandoned places, I guess we know the score.
Does anybody know what we are looking for?
...
The show must go on.
The show must go on.
Inside my heart is breaking.
My make-up may be flaking,
But my smile still stays on.

When I first listened to this song, I felt it deep in my gut. I felt as if I was Freddie writing this song, knowing I was sick and about to leave this earth without any knowledge of a purpose or reason for being alive in the first place. "Empty spaces, what are we living for? Does anybody know what we are looking for?" These are questions every human being asks at some point.

The line, "The show must go on...my smile still stays on," hits me the hardest. How many times in my life have I put a show on, just to make it through another day? How many of us do that? For those who have lived lives of trauma, this is our life, putting on a show. Many of us would not have made it this far without the ability to do so. It's an open secret that people who work in the mental health field—therapists, case managers, those who show up every day to help other people—have themselves been through some sort of trauma, which is why they show up. Many choose the field they are in because of experiences they have gone through in their own lives. I know that's part of why I did. Much like in the cycles of families, one person tries to help the others, to show the way, to heal the system, to prevent the suffering they know so intimately themselves, or help others heal from similar experiences, hoping to stop the cycle. Sadly, many of them have not fully healed themselves before doing so. I am a prime example of that. But there are those who have—I am thankful for finding an amazing therapist who has done the hard work of healing herself. You can always tell those who have done the work themselves—they are genuine, less ego centered, more authentic, and are not afraid to admit their shortcomings and flaws. They do their work from a strong, centered compassion. They know they can't rescue those in the healing process, but they can help guide others to engage the healing process within themselves. Healing is hard, so I do not say this to talk badly about anyone who has not walked this hard road, but there is a true difference between a healer that has done their own healing and one who has not. Both are beautiful souls doing hard work, but one has more capacity to help than the other.

For a long time, I felt that the saying "Fake it until you make it" was a positive saying. "Be strong! Push through! Don't show your feelings!" Who wants to be around a downer or cry baby? Who wants to listen to someone who always talks about their hard moments or sad things going on in their life? So I put on a mask and went on with the show. Behind closed doors at home I was a completely different person. Of course I knew how to do this because I had seen this happening in my parents' lives.

My stepdad was the ultimate "fake it" man. In public, everyone thought he was the kindest person, without a mean bone in his body, who would do anything for anyone. Behind closed doors, he was so mean, hateful, angry, and scary that none of us dared make a wrong move. We all knew that in public we had to "pretend" he was the perfect dad, but to avoid being beaten or yelled at I was constantly watching what I said, how I acted, and every movement I made. This man who was so scary at home, appeared in public to be nice, giving, gentle and kind. No one had a clue what kind of life the family was living in the home. We all learned how to put on a display, how to play a role in public—it became second nature for us. I am sure we all have our own perspectives on this—we each experienced it differently even though we all lived under the same roof.

For me, living with an abusive narcissist meant that everything had its place, and everyone had their place, and when something or someone was out of place, I knew it. To get out of place meant consequences, but I never knew what those might be. Would it be as easy as getting sent to my room, or getting yelled at, or given extra chores? That wasn't so bad. Or would it be getting beaten with a belt, or thrown across the room and called names? Would I need to protect my little brother? Or would it mean some form of sexual abuse that happened when no one was around, which I would have to keep a secret because I was told to not tell.

I wanted the other family members to stay in line too, because I feared what would happen to them—they were at risk of being harmed as well. Of course, none of us really knew what was going on with the other. I had no idea the extent of what was happening to my mom—I heard small snippets here and there, names he would call her, and other mistreatment. I saw things I did not want to see. I remember the first time I watched him beat her up. It was right after they married, when I was quite small. I was looking for her and when I looked out the front door of the house, I saw her in the front yard with him by the lawnmower. I watched as he grabbed her, threw her to the ground, and began to kick her and yell at her. I didn't understand what was happening. I had just gotten my mom back. My brother and I had been living with my granny and had just moved back in with our mom and this new man. I thought we would be building a new life, but here he was beating her up.

I can't recall a lot of my childhood. I believe I needed to block it out to survive. But I remember that day, hearing my mom in the laundry room crying after she had been beaten by my stepdad out in the yard. Wanting to help her, I went to the laundry room to ask if she was okay. She was on the floor, sitting in a pile of dirty laundry, crying. When I asked if she was okay, she became angry with me and waved for me to go away. I'm sure she was just wanting to protect me from seeing her like that, but I was hurt to the core. Having just seen my mom beaten, I was now— to my young mind—rejected by her on top of it. I don't remember anything about that day after that moment. I must have blocked it out, too painful to bear. I would see my mom crying like that many more times over the years because of how he treated her, each time pushing those feelings deeper into my body, keeping them there in the silence.

Things got worse after that day, for all of us. My brother pushed the limits and fought back even though he was too small to be successful. He often would laugh about it and I was terrified he would get more hurt because of it. I did my best to stay quiet and unseen, to avoid notice and thus avoid being hurt. All of us were trying our best to stay intact while the rest of the world, on the outside, saw a perfectly well put together family. My step-dad had money so my mom would get us nice clothing and my brother and I had many things we wanted or asked for. I believe this was a way she tried to show her love for us, giving us all the material things we wanted, helping us feel normal around our friends.

As I got older, I became overweight. By the second and third grade I was struggling to fit in with other kids in school. I didn't actually know that things at home were that bad, I just knew I didn't like it. I thought everyone's home life was like that. I certainly didn't know any different. "If you don't stop crying, I'll give you something to cry about." I knew it was true—we would be given something to cry about. All parents get mentally and physically tired and it is hard to meet the needs of a child twenty-four hours a day. It is exhausting, and a parent can say things they don't mean just to get through hard moments. Having had foster children and worked with kids for so many years, I understand how hard it is to be a parent. None of this is to make anyone feel bad for momentary lapses in judgment or self-control. We are human, we must give ourselves grace and allow room for that. But there are lines we must not cross.

I began to shut down. I stopped making friends. I spent recess sitting alone on the swings. Once in a while I would attempt to play with other kids on the playground, but nothing landed. I trained myself to hide my emotions. I taught myself how to behave in public, how to be good at home, how to push down feelings and move forward because "the show must go on."

42

Until recently, I did not understand the concept of feeling and how important it is. As a young child I remember having sadness and being afraid but always keeping quiet. The only times I would let myself feel sadness was when I was alone in my room, which is where I spent a lot of my time. It was my safe place, the only place I felt I could be truly me. Outside of that room I had to pretend. I had to pretend to be happy or okay. I had to interact with people I didn't want to, even though they were my family. The person I felt safest with was my little brother, but I also felt I needed to protect him. The small moments I remember easily from my early childhood are those spent with my brother, riding the bus home, and being with my granny.

Our first house was a split-level. To get to my room, you would go in the front door and up some stairs, then turning right, go down the hall—my room was the last one on the right. It was a corner room. Entering the room you would find my bed up against the left wall, a window slightly above it (facing south) and to the right, a dresser along the west wall. My closet was opposite the window, on the north side, in the corner diagonal to my bed. I would lay in my bed and look at my closet at night. I had a Cabbage Patch Kids pillow, Rainbow Bright sheets, and a night-light that I had gotten from my grandmother on my dresser. It was Mother Mary from the bible. I would turn it on every night before I went to bed to protect me. I vaguely remember hearing my parents yell at each other occasionally, but rarely were either of them home. It was mostly my granny who was there with my brother and me. My brother's room was right next to mine on the same side of the hall.

Many nights, I saw a shadow appear on my closet door. It had horns, a long face and snout, and long arms and legs. Kind of like a human with a huge bull's head. Sometimes the figure would move around my room, or float above my bed. It never hurt me, but I always felt afraid of it. One time I told my brother about it because none of the adults would believe me. They would tell me it was a shadow from my night light, or that something was just reflecting in my room. So, I asked my little brother to come and sleep with me one night to confirm that it was there. He must have around two or three years old. It is amazing to me that small children truly have an ability to understand and see things, unlike adults. That night he saw it also. Still to this day, if I ask him if I had a shadow in my room when I was little, he will confirm he saw it too. This wouldn't be the first "shadow" I saw in my life. I would see many of them as I got older. Maybe this was one of the reasons from a small age I felt I didn't fit in the world.

Shortly after that first shadowy visitation, Mom and Dad divorced. Dad moved out into a tiny apartment. For some reason I became terrified of him. He had a cot for me to sleep on when I went to visit him, and my brother would share the bed with him. But even in the cot beside his bed, I was terrified that he would touch me in some way. As I have moved through my therapy process, I have begun to understand my fear as a child. I started to pull out repressed memories of being molested as a small child by a neighborhood teenage boy. As I processed this, healing came, and I started to realize why I developed a fear of men, a fear of being taken advantage of, and a vigilant need to protect myself. I did not feel safe in the world, so I placed armor around myself to keep others out—even people who were safe. I was too young to understand the difference between safe people and unsafe people, yet it became the foundation I built my sense of self on, and from which that self-sense developed and continued throughout my adult life. I didn't have a clue where these fears came from until I started to heal from my trauma in my late 30s and early 40s.

In the 6th grade I started writing letters to one of my teachers, seeking connection and help. We had two 6th grade classes in different rooms. My teacher was kind but because I had to see her every day I didn't want to expose my secrets to her, so instead I wrote to the other class's teacher. She felt the safest to me. I never gave details about what was going on in my home, but I wrote about feeling alone. I wish I could go back and read some of those letters, to hear the voice of that innocent, struggling girl asking for help in the only way she could find.

I had been held back in the second grade, unable to fully grasp the concepts that were being taught. All the kids I had been with went up a grade while I stayed behind. Since then I had felt even more like the odd one out. At the end of each day we were required to spend time reading before the bus took us home. I remember my mind being so distracted I could not even see the words on the pages of the book—I just stared as though at blank paper. I put my chair up on my desk as we were instructed, so that the janitor could clean the floors that night, and I would walk around my desk in a circle, like an anxious animal waiting to be released, staring at the pages in the book. I would look up at the teacher once in a while to see if she was looking at me. Once when I felt her watching me, the heat rose in my face and I stopped walking, pretending with all my might to read. That same year, the teacher pulled me aside and told me I smelled bad, that I needed to bathe. I still remember her saying this to me. I had no idea I smelled. Maybe that was why I didn't have any friends? I still don't remember much about that time of my life, but I do remember that shortly after this, my mom moved us to my new step-dad's home and I changed schools.

My first clear memory of being sexually abused by my stepdad was the morning of Christmas Eve, my 6th grade year. I have vague memories of him coming to me in my sleep prior to that, but I believe I dissociated from my body to help me avoid the pain of it. That day, however, I was awake when it happened. On Christmas Eve I would go to my dad's house, so I was getting up and packing my bag, still in my pjs, a long shirt that went past my knees. I was twelve years old, had already started my period, and was developing breasts. He came into my room smelling of alcohol. It was early, maybe 8:30am. He began to say nice things to me and said how excited he was for it to be Christmas so he could give me some gifts. I was terrified. I didn't want any gifts from him, I just wanted him to leave my room. He closed the door leaving it slightly ajar, as he always did when he came in my room, just enough to make it appear as if he wasn't doing anything wrong. Then he came close, turned me so my back was facing him, and pulled me to him. He began to caress me and hug me from behind and touch me inappropriately. I was paralyzed by fear. I just stood there. I knew what was happening but I didn't know what to do. I tried to pretend it wasn't happening. The pungent smell of his alcoholic breath sickened me. I wanted to cry but nothing came out. Just then, my mom opened the door. He stopped, casually turned to her with a warm smile, and said he was giving me a Christmas morning hug. I smiled as well, pretending nothing was going on. She said something to me, probably something about getting ready for my dad to pick me up, and walked away. I can't tell you anything else about that morning or day other than 'the show went on.' I likely went to my dad's house, had Christmas with him, then went back to my mom's the next morning as though everything was okay, enjoying my Christmas, moving on with life as if nothing had happened the morning before.

Shortly after this experience, I was placed in a mental hospital for a while because I was depressed and suicidal. The social workers and my mom must have known something of what was causing my distress—they must have discussed the options, because they told me that if I mentioned anything abusive was happening in my home I would be removed and placed in foster care, never to see my family again. Did they think they were offering me a choice? I was terrified. I said nothing about what was

really going on or what had happened to me. My
silence became even more silent at that moment,
and my fear became stronger. But on the outside it
looked like I became stronger. I got a pass from the
hospital to visit my school. I felt like a stranger in a
strange land. I didn't fit in with any of the other kids
before this moment, and I sure didn't now. I didn't
even feel as if I fit in the chair. It was like I had
become a different person. I didn't know who to be in
the world. Before, I had been this shy, quiet girl,
easily camouflaged into the wall; now I felt like I was
being examined from all sides, the shameful secrets I
held within barely hidden from view. I needed to
figure out how to get the eyes off of me. No one in
the school but my teachers knew where or why I had
been gone for so long, and I never told anyone.
Maybe some of them figured it out eventually, as kids
do.

When I was in the hospital my stepmom gave
me a book about friendship. I still have it. I think it
was the first book I actually read front to cover. I did
struggle with making friends—everyone thought
that's why I was suffering. And of course, that was an
element of my experience. But really, it was because
I felt different, set apart. Especially after my hospital
stay.

From that moment on I got stronger on the outside, learned how to fake it, to wear a mask. One of the classes in the hospital was art therapy. We made a mask of our own face. I believe the purpose of this was to help us to take our mask off and expose what was under it. However, what I learned at that moment was how to put one on, a new one, a stronger one. I was vigilantly aware of how others saw me outside of my home, and I was determined not to go back to that place I had just been. I knew I was different and I knew what the consequences would be if I exposed the truth. So, I put a "better," stronger mask on. I had to become better than I was before I went to the hospital and that meant being happy even when I wasn't. I wasn't going to let anyone see that damaged part of me again, so I hid it more deeply. I had been changed, marked, set apart against my will. But I had control of how I appeared on the outside, and I worked hard at molding that image into an impenetrable armor. I even started to collect masks and hang them all over my room. Everyone was proud of me for my new, "better" mask.

As I got older, I looked around at how others fit themselves into the world—how did they do it? What did I need to do to fit in like them? I remember a distinct moment in which I thought about how I needed to start showing up differently than what I actually was. It happened one day while I was with my dad. My brother and I would go to his home every other weekend. On this day he had picked us up, asking the usual question, "How's school, Ang?" Because I didn't spend a ton of time with him, I didn't generally share much with him, so I said as usual, "Fine." He said, "Everything is always fine, with you." That stopped me. I had a physical sensation in my body as if something woke up, just a little. Before that moment, that answer had always worked and he would move on, never asking for more. This time, it didn't. I didn't know what to say next. I realized I couldn't count on that answer any more to deflect questions. People would continue to question me, and eventually I would have to say more about my life, which I certainly didn't want to do—I couldn't afford to share what was really going on. I clearly remember the shift in my mind, searching for the right language to use to share just enough but not too much. I decided the best defense was an offense, and just like that, I switched from being quiet and reserved to being a funny person that wasn't afraid to speak her mind. I decided that summer I was going to show up differently.

I began to exercise, getting up early every morning to run miles. I lost a lot of weight. Everyone was proud of me. I felt proud of myself too. I got better at sports. Now I felt the attention I had on me wasn't exposing my wounds and weakness, because what people saw were my athletic abilities. I kept working at it. In the evenings after school, I would go straight to the basketball court we had outside and play basketball for hours, improving my skills. This had the added benefit of keeping me out of the house and away from everyone. It was my time. Just me, my basketball, and the goal. Hours alone outside. I began to feel better about myself on the outside now that I had a way to function in the world, an acceptable identity that protected my inner pain from prying eyes—but the pain didn't go away, the wounds were not healing, just hidden.

By the time I was a junior In high school, my mother finally decided to divorce my stepdad. We moved and I changed schools. We were creating a new life, and I was happy to be in a safe home. I didn't know anyone in my new school, and because I had decided to be this new person in life, I was not going to miss any parties or chances to make new friends. I desperately wanted to "fit in" and be normal for once, and this was my chance. My old school had over 2,000 students, while the new one only had around 300, and only 69 in my class. Most of the parties were either at someone's home (usually mine) who had "cool parents" that would supply the alcohol, or at a house when parents were gone, or out in a field somewhere in the "boonies."

One Friday night I was hanging out with my friends on the softball team. We had a game the next morning and planned to stay the night together at one of the girls' houses and then go to the game together. This night, there was field party somewhere I hadn't been before. As was my habit, I drank a lot. I also smoked marijuana for the first time. The mixture wasn't in my favor—I felt off, not my usual "happy self," in fact I was feeling very depressed and didn't want to be there at all. My friends all seemed to be having a great time, laughing and enjoying themselves. Feeling disconnected from them, I stumbled over to a picnic table randomly placed out in the field and sat on top of it, my feet on the bench, drinking my beer and smoking a cigarette by myself. Looking out at the dark night, watching my friends have fun, I wondered if I would ever feel that way— care-free, enjoying life. I didn't feel like I ever would. I hated my life—a feeling that followed me everywhere. I compared myself to friends who appeared so easily to be themselves without fear. That night, I wasn't feeling good about myself.

As I sat there in this depressed state, a senior guy came up and sat beside me. I had seen him in the school but hadn't ever talked to him—I wasn't really interested in talking to anyone at the moment. But his attention felt good, soothing my despair. We talked a bit. Being drunk and high, I didn't think twice as he grabbed my hand, telling me he wanted to show me something. I had an uneasy feeling but didn't say anything, didn't say no, didn't stop him or myself. The hate I had for myself and my life, and the possibility of feeling something good, outweighed the feelings I had inside me that this was a bad idea. He led me down the field to a junkyard of sorts filled with a tumble of discarded cars all wrecked and broken down. I hadn't seen it there before that moment—I was confused and unsure of how far we had walked. My beer still in hand, I swigged the rest, hoping to numb myself and the feeling of uneasiness I was having. I didn't want to think about the position I was putting myself in. I didn't want to believe that once again someone would take advantage of me. I could feel what was about to happen. We both sat down and leaned against the tire of a broken car, talked some more. I thought maybe my fears were wrong, maybe he was just being nice.

And then he was on top of me. I was shaking my head no, trying to say it out loud but the words stuck.

I don't know if I managed to say it out loud or just thought it in my head. I wanted to cry, I wanted to fight. I was fighting him in my head, but after a bit I gave up and just let it happen. Once he finished, he tried to force me to give him oral and that is when I snapped awake from the dissociative state and pushed him away. He pulled up his pants angrily, grabbed his beer, and left me there on the ground, naked, without a word. I sat in the dark between the broken down cars as if I was just one more, discarded, wrecked beyond repair.

Finally I pulled my pants on. At some point I made my way back up to the party and found a friend I had come with. I told her, "I think I was just raped." I don't know what she said to me, I don't remember much after that other than riding in the back of a truck in the dark, wanting to shower, and then going to bed. All I knew was that I had to get up and go to the softball game the next day. In the morning I was completely numb, I had no energy to pretend, to put on the mask of a normal, fun-loving team-member, cheering, making noise and laughing. Someone later told me that my coach asked them what was wrong with me that day.

I can't remember how or when, but I must have become that outwardly happy girl again. It's what I did to get by: get back in line, get back to the show. Just shove down the pain, ignore it, push through. Follow the crowd, show up the way others want you to. It is just how you do life. No need to show anyone the inside of you that is hurting. When people ask how you are, it's always "good."

I had just begun to go to church not long before this incident. I didn't know much yet about the philosophy and beliefs of this particular church, but I liked the teachings about love—something I was searching for. About a week after I was raped, I told a friend from church about the experience. I'm not sure what I expected. I guess I hoped she would understand my pain and comfort me. But the reaction I got was unexpected, almost as wounding as the experience itself. She said that it was my fault for going to the party, drinking, and doing drugs. It was my fault for putting myself in that situation. Plus, she added, sex outside of marriage was a sin. I had caused the situation, I had sinned. Therefore, what I needed to do was repent.

I sat in shock. I had been hurt over and over in my life, but I never expected it to come from someone inside the church. That day, our friendship ended, never to be healed. We tried to repair our relationship later in life, but it just wasn't possible. I don't blame her now. We were young, she didn't know. It's hard for kids to know how to show up for other kids in their trauma. But I was looking in all the wrong places. I forgive her. Her response just came from the programming, the indoctrination of the church. That's all she knew.

Before joining the church, I had a best friend who was heavily involved in one and who would invite me to join her. I turned her down over and over. At that time I made fun of Christians, thinking they were weird, a little too "out there" for me. The music they listened to, the way they talked, the things they believed, all seemed weird. Plus, I enjoyed getting up on Sundays, watching TV, and reading my horoscope in the newspaper. But this friend would not stop asking me. So one day, when I was around 15 or 16, she asked me to go to a church camp. This time I finally gave in.

I don't remember much about the camp or what we did over the weekend except one thing. I was with a bunch of teenagers in a large room, maybe a barn. We were sitting on the floor, listening to someone talk. I don't remember the person or what they were talking about, but at the end of it, I was weeping. It was the first time I had cried in front of people. I never cried in front of people—I had always kept everything held tight inside. No one knew anything about my home life, what I had been through, what was going on. I was so embarrassed, I wanted to stop, but I couldn't. Before I knew it, a whole group of kids and adults were gathered around me, and they were happy. I didn't understand why they were so happy while I was crying. Then I was asked if I would accept the lord as my savior.

I thought, *How do I say no when all of them are surrounding me right now and so happy?* So I said yes. I followed along as they helped me recite the prayer, accepting Jesus into my heart. And BAM! I was a Christian. Just like that. All my sins forgiven. I assumed my life would get better and all the bad stuff would go away! When I got home from the weekend I told my mom I had become a Christian. She said, "Are you sure you want to do that?" We were standing in the kitchen. I didn't know if I wanted to be a Christian, but I did know I wanted my life to be better than it was. I wanted something else to happen—anything to change my fate.

Since I had been very young, I had seen shadows, had strange dreams, had feelings and sensations about things before they happened. Absorbing the church's teachings about demons and hell, I began to think of these phenomena from that perspective. They were caused by demons and the demons were what was making me feel so bad all the time. If I could cast them out, trusting in Jesus, I hoped my pain and negative thoughts would go away. I started to pray, asking God for help, writing my prayers down and describing all the strange experiences I had. Of course, all those bad feelings and thoughts did not go away, nor did the strange phenomena.

I know now, as I am healing, that it was not demons causing my pain, but real, visceral trauma. And I know as well that the dreams and visions and extra-sensory awareness are not caused by the devil, but are spiritual gifts. As a teenager however, I had no way to sort through these things, especially as alone as I was with it all. Seeing shadows, feeling the presence of things or beings not visible, sensing emotions of others, knowing that things were going to happen before they did and then finding out it was true. I joined the church hoping for a way to work with these things, make sense of them. From the perspective of the church's teachings, I determined that I was being possessed at times. I thought perhaps I could cast these demons out, asking God to deliver me, sometimes asking people to do deliverance sessions over me.

Later in my Christian studies I began to hear about things such as "gifts" of discernment and prophecy. This helped me consider that maybe these things didn't come from the dark or from Satan, but instead were just gifts. I had vivid dreams, would sense future events, tune in to energies and emotions in people. I still didn't tell a lot of people. Once, when I did share something about it with someone in the church, they told me I wasn't a mature enough Christian to use my gift. So I stayed silent.

I also didn't share my inner pain or traumas with anyone. I fully believed that I could just pray away all my negative thinking, sadness, and habits I had formed over the years because of my traumas. Of course, I didn't have a clue that most of my habits and struggles were developed as defenses against trauma. Instead, I thought I was this way because I was bad, sinful, and I needed to figure out how to be better, to be delivered from evil.

Then it happened, I had a sudden change that I now call my awakening.

The Awakening

It was the summer of 2016 and I was mowing my backyard. I had begun to feel uneasy about where I was in my life. My job, my current situations in general just didn't feel right. I felt something missing. I had been at the same job for years, the same church with the same people. I didn't especially dislike those things or those people. I just felt uneasy. I had a strange feeling there was more to life, that I was made for something different, something more. But what was it? What I questioned the most was my relationship with God. Was it real? Was all I had been taught and studied right? What is this thing called Christianity, and why is it a better religion than

61

all the others in the world? Why this one? Is the Bible real?

I had always felt I wasn't good enough. I didn't believe I was worthy of a life of success or love. I had dreams and ideas, but couldn't picture myself as someone who could accomplish them. I couldn't even live up to the person I was trying to be currently— why would I ever be the person I dreamed of being? I strived constantly just to have the little I did, and to be okay with myself. That day, in my backyard, those same thoughts went through my head, mowing the same direction I always mowed. Thoughts of self-doubt, defeat, an uneasy feeling that I would never get it right floated through and around my head like biting insects. Prayers of repentance of my many sins constantly repeated over and over. Ruminating over all the things I did wrong the day before and all the things I'd said and done wrong to other people in the past; everything I couldn't seem to get right in life, the things I messed up or didn't seem to be able to overcome. I was a sinner, and I needed to be cleansed. Something always seemed to be wrong with me. I would show up on Sunday mornings and feel like filth, as if I needed to wash myself with the words of the bible and stand in church and be cleansed. I dared not miss a church service because I would miss getting my time in with God, with His people, and then would have to find a way to make up for it. Constantly striving.

That day was no different. The same feelings, same thoughts went through my head. I had no idea my own trauma held me in a shame spiral causing me to curse my own life, believing I had no value, manifesting negative beliefs about myself and my life. Adding the religious beliefs and teachings on top only amplified my thoughts of self-defeat and doubt. On this particular day, I was chewing on all of this as always, just a normal day. Then a voice, barely audible, spoke in my head.

I am not sure if it was God, or an angel, or one of my spirit guides, but I heard a voice. This is what I would describe as my awakening moment—meeting the real God, the one I had been seeking all my life. In that single moment, I had my first encounter with what I would call true love. My spirit awakened.

I had heard of other people having awakenings and I always wondered what it was like. Thirteen years prior to this, in 2003, I had a strange experience when a man hugged me and I felt actual lightning bolts go through my body. It was in the church setting, and when I felt the energy go through my body, I fell to the ground, stunned. It scared me so much I jumped up and yelled at the man, asking him what he had done to me. He just smiled and laughed and explained to me it was God, "the filling of the Holy Spirit."

Now I understand that everything is energy, and I know that it was, indeed, God. It was a divine experience where God's love energy came into me. I don't know if it was placed in me for a reason, or a gifting, or any purpose other than for me to feel it. But I do know it happened, and I still remember the actual feeling of the energy going into my body. I will never forget that moment.

This time, it was as if that same energy was actually speaking to me, an audible voice talking to me from Heaven. Sometimes when asked how they know something or why they believe in something, people will say things like, "I know that I know." After my experience on this day, I understand what they mean. I know that I know. This happened to me. There is no denying it. A clear change happened in me at that moment.

Some of the things I have experienced since then would be considered heretical in the setting of the church. I have spent significant time in many different church settings of various denominations, both in the USA and overseas—non-Denominational Churches, Catholic, Lutheran, Nazarene, Church of

God, Baptist, and the one I spent the most time in was Charismatic Pentecostal. I attended a Christian College, studied the bible in depth, attended Missionary schools. I am well educated in the bible, have an Associate Degree in Bible, and can quote bible verses by heart. I can tell you who Jesus' brother is, who the twelve disciples are, and what books Paul wrote. I can tell you where to look for certain verses in the bible, and reference the author of a given verse. I was a Christian to the core. I accepted Jesus many times, and understood that I had to be "reborn" again through him to go to heaven. I repented from my sins daily, I prayed, I had quiet times, I went to bible studies groups, women's groups, I taught women's groups, taught Sunday School, taught youth ministry, went on missions trips. The striving, the seeking, the wanting to know God and be known by him was real. I know how a religious minded Christian thinks, especially when it comes to someone who no longer follows the faith and leaves the church. I myself judged people who left, thinking that they never really knew Jesus, never really followed him as their savior. So you can be sure, that day, I was shaken to the core, hearing this voice inside telling me I was striving in the wrong direction.

I stopped, took my hands off the mower and turned it off. The voice said simply, "You're doing it wrong, stop walking in Condemnation." In that moment, everything I knew was shaken loose and stripped away, all my beliefs fell away, all my thinking dissolved into dust, as though a cyclone had whirled around inside me leaving me empty, silent. "Stop walking in condemnation," is a teaching from the Christian faith I was striving for. I knew the words well. I had even taught them before in my Sunday school and in women's studies. But now, as the words arose in my mind, they carried an entirely different significance. I wondered why I was hearing this now? What did this mean for me? What was I doing to walk in condemnation?

I asked the voice, "What do you mean? How am I walking in condemnation?"

Visions started to flow through my mind: visions of myself striving to be good enough, striving to be someone other than myself. I saw the leaf vision again, looking down from above, watching that leaf striving to get around that rock, fighting against the stream of life—that was me, trying to be perfect, working to be the best version of myself, trying to find my place in the world, trying to cram all the different parts of myself into one, neat, tidy place. Everything in my life had a place, including everything in my house, my car, my behaviors, my feelings, my humanity, everything had to be contained and controlled. I was afraid to listen to music that went against my religious teaching; everything I did was carefully thought out and chosen to hold up this version of myself I thought I needed to be and to protect myself from "demonic activity." Rather than religion freeing me from the pain and fear caused by the traumas in my life, it fueled them and amplified them. The teachings insisted I had to be afraid of myself and my impulses, that I had to be vigilantly on guard against sin in myself. This kept me in the loop of fear and self-condemnation.

Then the visions shifted to memoires of myself once enjoying music as a teen before I became "religious"; dancing in my car with my friends, feeling free to be myself, to have energy alive in my body, to be expressive. Well, not entirely free—I was living inside the protective behaviors of trauma by then, but free of the additional constraints of religion.

Standing at the lawn-mower in the middle of my yard, my life flashed before my eyes, and everything came to a halt. I stood there completely still, lost without an anchor, without direction. *Do I really let go of all I've been taught through the religious life I've*

been living? I knew in my gut the answer was yes.
How do I even start this process? That night I had a vivid dream.

I saw myself leaving my church, my job, and everything familiar about my life at the time. I saw myself starting my own business and beginning a whole new life. Hopes and desires I had once dismissed because I never thought I would be good enough arose distinctly in my mind's eye. I suddenly felt as if I could actually do them. The next morning, I knew I needed to take a step forward in the direction I had been shown. The change would be massive, overwhelming to do all at once, so the first thing I decided to do was to let go of the Christian music.

As I reached to turn the channel on the radio in my car, I was besieged by religious fears and thoughts that I was inviting demonic activity into my life. I had to push through these fears and thoughts, like a crowd of zombies in my head, but I did it. I turned the dial to a station that was playing a song I once loved. My heart relaxed—the zombies fell back. It was like I was going back to my authentic self for the first time in my life. Finding who I really was. For years I had to fight these thoughts each time I started to change a part of my mindset I had developed in religion. I had no idea how much extra trauma religion had brought into my life, how deep and powerful the programming was that had developed in my mind.

I didn't know it then, but I do now: that was the beginning, the awakening of my true spiritual journey. I think one of the hardest things about losing religion is transforming the part of the mind that has been so deeply conditioned and trained. It doesn't change overnight. The same is true when you are working through trauma. The thoughts, attitudes, beliefs, and habitual emotions we have are all supported by neural pathways in the brain and throughout the body. To change those takes work, conscious effort, and time.

I was working through both types of conditioning at the same time. As I would adjust one behavior that came from my religious programming, I would notice underneath it patterns that came from my earlier life growing up in an abusive home. I started to see patterns in my life that I had been holding onto since childhood, things I believed about myself and others because of both trauma and religion. I knew that both needed to be healed. One of the main programs my mind had developed was a fear of abandonment. I had been in therapy many times throughout life, but I hadn't addressed these things very deeply. I never talked about the hard issues, things I faced as a child, teen, or even young adult. Early in my process I could only hit the surface level issues, or certain select things that I could remember. As my mind changed and religion slowly stopped holding onto my thoughts, I began to open myself to new ways of healing my mind. My values were changing, and I started to try new things that I once saw as evil—things such as meditation, yoga, grounding in nature, crystals, energy healing and reading, hearing the spirit and spirit guides. All things I once was terrified of.

I always had a very close connection to the Divine. I remember as a child, before I even really knew much about God, or anything religious, I had a connection with energy, what I now refer to as God's energy. I clearly remember as a very young girl, maybe around the age of four or five, sitting in the bathroom looking at a scrape on my leg, and thinking to myself that I was going to ask God to heal it. I had never heard of "healing energy," or "laying on of hands," or knew that it was something done in a charismatic church or Pentecostal church. I knew nothing of these things. I just had this feeling I could ask something bigger than myself to do it. I sat there and innocently asked this source I knew in my heart, which was bigger than myself, to heal that scrape on my leg. I repeated my request over and over, patiently waiting and trusting, and I remember sitting there and watching it disappear. I wasn't surprised or elated. I just knew it would happen if I asked, and I went on with my life. I'm pretty sure I didn't tell anyone it happened. I forgot about it for many years until my recent years of awakening spiritually.

Over the years of growing in my relationship with God—including my years in the church and once I left the church—I began to develop a sense of knowing. I was able to pick up on things being said when I wasn't present, or the energy of what was going to happen, or even what had happened. The bible would call this a prophet. I am unsure what I would call it now that I have left the church. Maybe an energy reader. Maybe it doesn't need a label. We label things so we can make sense of them. But for now all I know is that when I am in my true self, I sense things. Some things I get right, others I get wrong. I have come to understand that the times I am wrong, I am often thinking in my trauma mind or ego mind. But I am learning to not judge myself— judgment is the ego self fighting against the spiritual. And that is often what religion causes people to do. The important thing is to stay open and able to learn.

I get a sense of things and often know things before they happen or before someone tells me something. I can tell someone is hiding something from me, sense energies shifting in a room, or if they have done something they feel shameful about or are sending out something negative towards me or someone else. I also can feel or hear if they are about to enter a season of change in their life, or if they need to be warned about something. I get that for myself too. I don't always listen to this, mostly I think because change can be hard, or because I don't always want to know. But, as I am awakening to my spirit, my higher self, I am starting to learn to be a little more aware of it, and a bit more quick to listen.

If you have spent any time around religion, or even around people who are spiritual, you will hear things such as, "we are spiritual beings," or "we are spirits living in a human life." I have always agreed with this on an intellectual level, but I never really connected with it until recently. In my previous religious thinking I understood that for my spirit to go to heaven I had to be good enough in my earthly human body. I had to strive to do all things right and live the best life I could. I had to have all my life in the right place, not commit the sins that would keep me from entering heaven.

In my new growth, I have come to understand there are two parts of us: the Ego, which is our human self, and the Spirit, which we can also call our Soul. I have come to believe that God is Energy. God is the energy ALL around and in us: in the nature around us, in the people around us (both those we consider good and those we think of as bad), God is in all, the dirt we stand on, the air we breathe, the objects and particles we can see and the things we cannot see. God is everywhere. I do believe that Jesus walked the earth as well.

For a while, I wasn't sure. When my dad died in September 2020, my faith was forcefully challenged and I had many destructive thoughts. I was already internally deconstructing my religious and trauma conditioning. When he died, I really began to wonder. Where did he go? What was he now? What about his body, what about this life he lived? So many questions. Being left behind, having to process his absence from my life was even harder without the religious structure I once would have turned to for solace. I had been taught that at judgment day, Jesus would return to the earth, take up all the dead bodies, resurrect them as he was resurrected, and reunite them with our spirits to live with Jesus and God forever. But our family cremated my dad's body. Cremation destroys the body that would supposedly be resurrected. I find it odd that an old body, turned to ash or decayed into dirt, would be recreated and lived in again. I would rather have a new one if I am going to have to live in a body again! However, I am not sure I believe I will be going into a body again, or if there is a resurrection, or even a day that Jesus will return. Everything I have experienced since my awakening has gone completely against those teachings. I have come to a deeper understanding of God's love, and what our spirits truly are here and now—not in some distant future.

In searching for an answer to the question of where my dad was after death, and what he was now, I finally landed on the conclusion that he simply is. He is a spirit. Just as Jesus would say, "I am, that I am," my dad is now an "I am." He is within the energy of God. He is with the spirit of Jesus as well as all of the spirits that have gone before us, and all the love energy of the universe. He is also with me. He is energy. He can still see me, communicate with me (in his own ways of course), and he still has life, even more abundantly than he did on earth. Our true lives are not really our bodies; life is our spirit. When we disconnect from our body, we live outside of this 3D world, the matrix we are stuck in currently, which is only what we can see with our physical, human eyes. Everything we physically see with our naked human eye is not all that is truly there. From a spiritual view there is a vast reality beyond anything we can even imagine.

Once we step into our true, divine self, we see through our spiritual eyes and into the spiritual realm. Within the spiritual realm we see in what could be called 5D, the true spirit self. This is like the innards of the computer that makes up what we are currently seeing. That is our true being, our true energy. It is almost like going into the inner world of a computer when we move into our true self. The spiritual realm is so un-comprehensible to our human mind that the only way we can connect with it is by getting out of our ego, and that requires quieting our mind. This is not an easy task for anyone and requires much discipline and practice. Some may obtain it more easily than others, and trauma can create an even greater obstacle. Quieting the mind can expose feelings and sensations held under the surface by daily activity and thought. That can cause triggers for those with unprocessed trauma, bringing up shame, anger, fear, even terror. We humans are used to constant stimulation and information filling our environments and heads, buffering us from what lies beneath the surface, and we rarely spend moments in intentional silence. Either a TV or radio is on, or we are surfing the internet, or we are surrounded by other people. Meditation takes us out of this stream of activity, allowing the mind to still, and our whole being to collect itself. Meditation can help us to see ourselves more clearly, to have compassion for ourselves, and to relax our grip on the "act," the "persona" that we use to shield ourselves from ourselves and from the world. This is why meditation is often used to decrease our ego, relax our defenses, so we can connect with our higher selves.

Mediation is a discipline that has been used for many centuries and in many traditions. I have found meditation to be more effective for me than prayer was when I was a practicing Christian. It has been easier for me to connect with God and my higher source of love and spirit than I ever was when I tried to pray before. When I would pray, I would often strive to obtain a quiet mind, but I did not know how to get to that point of true silence where I could hear from God. Religion often makes prayer about the ego-self, about striving for perfection, about obtaining things, about survival. In my meditation practice I have sometimes found myself taking this striving approach, striving to obtain quiet or connect with energy. The ego mind tries to do the work of the spirit self, but it always falls flat. These can be very humbling moments for me. I have been moved to tears of despair, finding myself trapped in striving and seeking instead of just being. In my meditations, my practice is to deconstruct my mind, to rewire and retrain it to let go of the striving and instead to open, relax, and receive the spiritual energy that comes from a higher level of being. IN the church I was warned against opening to such energies, as they were deemed to be of the devil, so I have experienced fear arise as I open myself this way. But what I have found in this relaxation and surrender is humility, love, and healing.

In the church I was taught to stay away from meditation or connection to the spiritual world—these connections were called "new age" or at times "demonic." However, I have come to realize that there really is nothing "new" about any of it, and certainly nothing demonic. I believe that somewhere along the development of Christian teachings someone realized that if people were to connect with their higher selves they would realize they did not need the church or even religion at all to connect with God. They would discover that all the following, striving, and obeying had no relevance to connecting to a higher self and to love energy. If this were to happen, the powers of hierarchical systems would lose their authority and there would no longer be a way to control and influence the masses. I do believe some of the teachings of the church and religion have good qualities and some of the bible is correct. But over the centuries religion has developed into a system for socialization and power, not about love energy and helping people connect with their higher selves. Teaching the concepts of quieting the mind, decreasing the need to strive and obey, leaning more into loving oneself first, and then coming into connection with the spirit by developing a higher consciousness—these are concepts that were brought into the world by those who first walked with God. Over time they have been usurped by the demands of ego and mind to regain control and power. I believe those who walked the earth in the beginning knew their true divine selves most intimately, and knew how to connect with God on a visceral level. I also believe that we are seeing a movement in which more and more people are coming to the awareness of this true self, this true nature, and many are awakening once again to their divine potential.

As I have grown over the years in my awakening process, deconstructing my thoughts, I have opened myself to new ways of connecting with the divine and highest source of energy. I have developed abilities to meditate longer, understand how to connect with my higher self, listen to my intuition, tap into my spirit and psychic abilities, and hear the spirit of God on a much more divine level than I ever was when I was in religion. This has given me the ability to see the world around me in a much different way as well, to connect with nature, with spirits, talk with angels and even see them, meet my spirit guides, and have a relationship with my dad. I would say that I have a better relationship with my dad now than I did when he walked this earth. I don't know if I'll ever have a full understanding of these gifts and abilities, and honestly, if I ever feel that I have, I think pride would creep in, and I never want that. I believe that staying humble is of vital importance, and I always want to be growing and learning more, while keeping my ego small, and letting my spirit lead. I never want to be someone who thinks they know all truths in life. If I did there would be no reason to continue to seek truth in this life or even connect with the things I mentioned above. Obtaining all the knowing of the universe would leave no reason to truly live life. So I fully admit that I am still exploring my understanding of many things. My heart's desire is to be love, light, and radiate positive energy into the universe to help others find their way to the true source of the divine energy of love, which I call God, and to help them know that they can also heal.

I will always remain open, willing, and ready to learn more. Being ready to hear from my spirit guides, my dad, those who have gone before me, from Jesus, from angels, and from God, the divine love energy itself. I will not judge where I am at any point, because I have come to understand that the judgment we believe God places on us is entirely made up in our minds. I work to eliminate that kind of thinking. Nothing about my spiritual awakening was something I could have known ahead of time or intentionally sought out. It just happened. I cannot tell you why, I cannot tell you what made it happen that day, or even why it happened in the way it did. But I can tell you that I was seeking the truth wholeheartedly. Maybe that was what allowed God to come to me and speak to me that day. I believe that I was calling on the energy of love to manifest that day, without even knowing it. I wanted a higher connection with God, with my spirit, and with my gifts. I wanted to be all I was supposed to be and I didn't want to spend the rest of my life wandering and wondering. I think in my wholehearted desire for truth, my spirit was able to come to the surface and lead me, and somehow I was able to fall back into the stream of energy that is life, like a leaf falling in a stream, and rest and trust in that flow to take me to the next rock in life, which led me to my healing process.

The Leaf Lesson,

Leaving the Line

When I was in the church, I was taught it was virtuous to deny myself, to put others first, to turn the other cheek, to love my neighbor. It wasn't hard for me to put others first, to sit back and stay in the background, and to consider myself last. I already had a scarcity mindset I had developed in my childhood—it was not hard to connect these new teachings with my habits of shutting down my mind and silencing my voice. These teachings simply confirmed the wisdom of doing what I had already been doing. I had already been shrinking myself my whole life. I had no idea how to choose myself. I had no idea how to set a boundary or how to say no when

I didn't want to do something. My lack of self-worth was so reliable that everyone knew I would be the one that showed up to help with things. I was always there to help! There was never a "no" that came from my mouth. In fact, I would volunteer!

I followed right in line with what everyone wanted me to do, and I did it believing I was doing it for the sake of others and obeying God. I was earning my love, I was earning my place in heaven, I was earning my badge to be a strong Christian woman, to be seen as someone worthy. I thought it might take a long time because I was so damaged, so much of a sinner. Being last was never a problem for me though. Being patient was easy. I was always willing to give, and if I was seen as anything other than nice, kind, giving or loving, I panicked! I needed people to see me as a good person all the time. If I wasn't seen as a good person, I became anxious that my salvation was on the line. I did everything I could to fix it. I even became angry about it.

Someone from a trauma background doesn't have a problem believing they should be last. It is believing in themselves as valuable they have a problem with. Learning to value myself was the first lesson I really needed to learn. Maybe I didn't understand the teachings properly—maybe they

didn't mean to demean oneself or neglect oneself—
but that was how I understood the teachings because
it fit perfectly with my trauma, and being told I would
go to hell if I didn't obey the teachings just added fuel
to the fire that I needed to fix myself up or I'd be in
big trouble.

I find traffic jams highly symbolic of human
behavior. Have you ever been in a long line of
stopped cars, wondering what was happening way
up in front to cause such a block? Sometimes one
car will go driving past in the other lane, seeming to
ignore their place in the line, arrogantly assuming
they can drive around the rest of us. I'd always been
afraid to do that. I always assumed there was a good
reason everyone was stopped, and I obediently
stayed in line, waiting. Then sometimes, when I've
been driving the opposite way from a long traffic jam,
I notice that all that is holding the line up is one small
car, maybe with a flat tire, pulled over to the side, but
no one in that long line knows what is happening up
front, so they all wait. Everyone assumes that if
everyone else is stopped there must be a good
reason and they stay stopped too. At some point, one
car decides to slow down or stop, then another, and
another, and before anyone behind them knows why,
a line is created and maintained by simple
association.

Most of us are more worried about what others think than what we feel in our guts we should do. Somewhere over our lifetime we lost the ability to go inward and trust our intuition, instead holding back in fear, not daring to break out of the lines formed by others. It happens slowly over time and eventually feels quite natural. I remember being on a highway sitting in one of those traffic jams. As the line formed behind me, I began to wonder what was up front. Should I risk going around it? What if it is something bad and I get up there and regret it? What if I get myself in trouble and can't get back to my route? On the other hand, I thought, What if I sit here for twenty or thirty minutes, or an hour, waiting, and finally get to the front and notice that at any point I could have just gone around? That day, I did it. I took the risk. It was scary yet liberating! I had fears of what everyone else was thinking about me. But I did it! Sure enough, at the beginning of the line was a stalled car on the side of the road. I had avoided sitting there for an hour, and was free to go on my way!

Something amazing happened after that. As I pulled out of line and began to drive freely, I noticed others started to do the same. One by one, cars pulled out of the line, driving around it and continuing merrily on their way. By making my own choice, I gave others permission to do the same. We all started to become unstuck from an imaginary jam started by one unfortunate person who actually was stuck. A belief formed that we all must be in this line because someone else had to slow down or stop. But their situation was their truth they needed to live by in that moment—a real circumstance. By misinterpreting their situation for ours we all got slowed down, stuck, held back. Meanwhile, sitting and waiting, so many people trusting the line, all it took was one person to step out and take the lead. All I had to do was trust my gut, my sense that maybe there wasn't anything bad up there, and be willing to take the risk.

That day was a highly symbolic part of my journey and the process of breaking off or letting go of many things holding me back—the many thoughts I had formed over the years that trapped my mind and caused me to live in fear; being in line with what others had taught me because I was afraid to step out of line; the thoughts of hell, the thoughts of messing up, making one wrong step, saying the wrong thing, not being good enough or doing enough. It was such a trap, a self-sustaining system of defeat. The structural brain washing that I was caught up in convinced me that taking one step out of line would signal my doom. However, there was something in me that awoke. It was as if my inner essence was coming back to life. The little girl, still innocent, who could sense and see things. As I said in previous chapters, I always knew there was something different about me. As a result of trauma and religious training, I had lost that part of myself. But that day, the day I got out of line, something started to come back, my spirit came alive again.

I spent most of my younger life seeking out ways to feel safe. I remember as a very young girl, around the age of three, having visions of angels climbing down a ladder to my window by my bed, then coming in and helping me out the window to climb back to heaven. I knew that was where I came from. I knew it was safe there, that nothing bad would happen to me there. I longed to be back in the safety of my true home. During my hypnotherapy sessions I went into some dark places of trauma I experienced in childhood. I think as adults we believe we can forget things. But we don't. It is easy to believe that we can cover things up by drinking them away, working them away, or doing enough good in the world that we make up for the bad. I thought that for a while; I went down that path a few times, but like I said, I always knew something was calling me out of it.

There are two ways people hide from their trauma. One is by withdrawing and avoiding things that trigger it, and the other is through external performance and behaviors to overcompensate for it. I think I did both. Maybe that gave me an ability to understand both sides, so now I can help people heal from these things as well.

One who comes from trauma can move into addictions or extreme behaviors of many kinds. It is hard for those living in a trauma response to find balance. From a young age, food became a comfort to me. Eating was a way I could escape. When I would eat, I felt safe and able to ignore other things happening in and around me because I could focus on the food and the sensations I had eating the food. Sometimes I would eat so much I would make myself sick. I clearly remember being so sad once in my twenties, but all I could think about was getting a box of donuts. The thought would not leave and it seemed as if it was in control of me. I viscerally felt I had to obey it. I got in my car and went to the store to get the donuts. I also bought some other items so it did not appear as if that was all I was getting, and I went back home. I know I did not set out to eat the whole box. I lay on my couch watching a movie, and slowly ate one donut, then another, and another. Between each donut, I sat the box in the kitchen, thinking it would be my last. Then once again I had the box in front of me, watching and eating, until I was down to the last one, and what the heck, I ate that one too. Twelve donuts. A dozen. I ate a whole dozen donuts, by myself, in one sitting.

Let's talk about shame. The shame I felt immediately after I did this. I hated myself before this moment, but as soon as I did it, I hated myself even more. The donuts did not make me feel better at all. They made me feel worse. While I was eating them, I was able to ignore all my feelings. But as soon as they were gone, all the feelings came back, and more. This is the same with other addictions such as drinking or drugs. Alcohol is one of the worst addictions out there because it is so widely accepted and seen as "fun" and what you do when you get together with your friends. You are often seen as an outcast or odd one out if you do not engage in it. Before you know it, you are drunk, maybe even unable to remember the evening or what happened. Over time our bodies adjust to the amount of alcohol we ingest and we end up needing more and more of it to obtain the feeling of numbness. When we don't have it, we feel more and more hollow and uncomfortable. Before we realize it, the amount we had before does not cause us to feel numb or drunk, and then we end up needing more and more to just feel normal. Most addictions are like this. Which is why I ended up having twelve donuts that day instead of just one and being satisfied.

I didn't realize that I had an addiction to alcohol until a very good friend pointed it out to me shortly after my dad passed away in September 2020. Unknowingly, I had turned to drinking to cope. I am so thankful for this friend. I know this was a divine set up for her to step in for me. It was only within a month of my dad's death that she pointed this out to me and I quickly was able to see what she saw. She also saw something in herself she wanted to change, and began the journey with me. With her support, I felt as if I could work on stopping. I know this friend didn't continue the journey after we both decided to stop drinking together, but it was a pivotal point for me. I believe that one of the reasons it was easy for me to continue my journey was because I was also working on my spiritual awakening process. But had she not made the decision to quit drinking herself, I might not have been able to look myself in the mirror and see my own problem. I didn't even know I had so much alcohol in my home. When I was able to actually look in the mirror without looking away and ignoring what I saw, I was able to see myself going down a dark road and it needed to be stopped. Just like the food addiction I had. That fall, in 2020, I poured all my alcohol out in the sink, and never looked back. I tried to engage in drinking again a few times that year, thinking that one here and one there wouldn't be bad, I didn't mind having a few with friends occasionally. But I never felt fulfilled when I did or as if I could show up as my best authentic self. It just felt like a cover to fit into the "line" of life. I'm not saying it is wrong to have a drink, or a glass of wine with a friend or a night out at dinner. When you are in control of your life, there is nothing wrong with those things. There is also nothing wrong with eating a donut. But when you've come from any form of trauma, whether you consider it trauma or not, addictive coping behaviors can easily begin to control your life, and if you haven't dealt with it, that is when you must take a hard look at what you are trying to hide from. What feeling are you covering up? Have you allowed a behavior to form into an addiction or developed an addictive personality? The main thing is to be aware of your why.

Something clicked for me when my friend pointed this out to me, and I haven't gone back. I'm not sure I will, and I really have no desire to do so. That "line" is not one I want to be in any longer. Nor the fast-food restaurant, buying a box of donuts, trying to fill that pain with food line. Now I know it was just my inner child looking for someone to hold her and tell her she was okay. The temporary brain chemistry that junk food or other substances give are a poor substitute for the real chemistry of love and safety. Learning who you really are and what you really need is the first step, digging into the reason you are sitting in that line—whatever line it might be. Then you must find out what really fills your spirit and soul.

Most of my trauma happened between the ages of three to seventeen, and then again in my twenties I experienced a few things that left me feeling defeated and shameful. In my late thirties and forties my healing began. The trauma I experienced included many different kinds of harm—emotional, physical, sexual, some neglect and abandonment at times. Trauma can be experienced in many ways. It doesn't have to be the most dramatic life experience. It can be something as simple as feeling as if you don't live up to your parents' expectations. Trauma can be that small thing that no one knows about, or the big thing that no one knows about. The world tends to put labels on experiences and we often listen to them, believing that one experience is worse than another. But trauma is anything that disconnects you from your true self. It self-perpetuates because the defenses we put in place to protect our fragile young selves, later serve to keep us separated from our true selves. Thus the vicious circle continues.

91

It isn't the exact experience that determines the severity of the trauma, it is how it made you feel and what you had to do to survive it. If you went through a horrible storm as a child and it still bothers you each time it storms, that indicates trauma. The experience may have formed some networks in your brain that caused you to start to think and feel differently. Maybe when it stormed, your parents had you go to your room alone and you felt abandoned. Now each time it storms, you have a reaction of feeling abandoned. Or maybe, you have a hard time forming connections with others in life because you are always worried about being told to go away. As you see, something as simple as being told to go to your room at a certain time can be traumatic to someone, and yet to another person it can seem insignificant.

For a myriad of reasons we do not share these types of experiences with others, holding them deep inside instead. Maybe you were too ashamed to share an experience with someone, maybe you were told not to share it with anyone, maybe you didn't know it was trauma, or you were dissociated at the time and don't remember it. Whatever the reason, holding the experiences inside, and the feelings associated with the experiences, keeps them in place and has an effect on physical as well as emotional wellbeing. You hold it in your body all your life, and

now don't understand certain irrational reactions you
experiences as an adult.

Maybe you do remember it and have no idea
how to tell people about it because it seems so
insignificant to you in comparison to someone else's
trauma about being raped or having a loved one
murdered. Or, maybe you experienced something,
told someone, and they did not believe you and you
vowed to never tell anyone again. Whatever the
experience was, if it was significant enough that you
began to think differently about yourself or the world
around you, it was trauma. If you have a phobia, or
fear, or struggle with connection or relationships of
any kind, it can be caused by trauma. Don't assume
that because your experience wasn't as "severe" as
someone else's, your story doesn't matter. It does.
Your trauma matters because it is yours. It doesn't
matter what anyone else thinks. Never compare your
experience with someone else's and never let
someone try to compare your story with someone
else's either. Your story is yours.

Whatever experience you have had in your life, it
is up to you to heal from it. No one else can do that
part for you. We are given this opportunity of life to
use it for a purpose. I fully believe we are on this
planet for a reason. All of us! Not one of us is here

because we are meant to sit in the line and follow someone else or do someone else's job. Maybe what we do will be similar to someone else, and we will work alongside them, but no one has the same DNA as you, and no one has the same fingerprint as you, nor the same eyes to look through, and that is on purpose. No one has the same spirit as you either. The vibration of love you carry in this world cannot be duplicated or re-created. If you do not live up to your calling, no one else can. Yes, it is true that if you decide not to step into it, someone else will move into that place, but they will not be you doing it, or do it the way you can do it. What you do will never look like what someone else does. Someone else will never have my story, and I will never have yours. People may experience many things very similar to what I have experienced, but their perspective of it, their understanding of it, how they manage it and deal with it, heal from it, and then learn from it, will be different.

If you look at trees closely, you will see that no two are the same. There are many in a forest, but none of them have the exact same branches, the same leaves, the same bark, the same shade they provide. None of them take from the same part of the sun. No matter how many of them grow in a forest, not a single tree is the same tree. They may be the same type and live right beside each other, but none of them will grow to look like each other. One may grow taller, one may grow wider., they'll have different shapes altogether, each having its own unique inner workings. You will find in a forest that a tree never waits for another tree to catch up as it is growing. Trees grow because that is what they are meant to do—to reach for the sky, to find the sun, to manifest the leaves to provide shade and nourishment for those under it, and then in the fall, shed those leaves only to compost them back into the earth to nourish the ground, plants and even itself again.

Each tree also supports the others, and receives nourishment and support from the others. In the process of supporting other trees, they don't lose their independence though. They don't start to shape shift or look like the tree beside them. As they grow, some trees may latch on to other trees' roots to help steady themselves, which allows them to help each other grow, giving one another nourishment, sharing resources, and warning each other of predators. Others grow independently but they often don't fare as well as those who grow interdependently. Trees dig their roots deep into the soil of the earth to make sure they are firmly connected and ready for any storm that may come. Living together in a forest ensures they are supported as they have the protection of each other. But even with all this obvious interdependence and reciprocal support, you will notice one tree never waits for another tree to grow first. It just grows. I believe that is what we humans are meant to do on this earth as well. By being our authentic selves, valuing ourselves, we actually are more able to benefit others and become a reliable member of the whole.

We are not meant to do this life on earth alone. At times we need help or someone to push us forward when we are stuck. To really have an awakening process in life may involve heartache, and sometimes it is a devastating or life altering event that propels us towards our healing. Finding our potential and purpose often comes after some of the darkest moments in life. But what I want you to understand is that we each have an individual purpose.

Most humans spend their lives waiting for someone to come and help them find that purpose, to save them, to help them get up and reach for the sun, never realizing that they are responsible for digging into the dirt themselves, and from that, they can manifest their own growth. It is in the dirt that we grow. It is in the dirt that we find nourishment. For so long, I wanted to avoid my wounds and scars, ignoring and denying experiences that had happened in my life. But it was only when I finally dug into it the dirt of my life that I finally began to understand that I was the one that was going to save myself.

Of course I also needed help, and I have many people who nourish and support me; I have an amazing therapist that helps guide and lead me in the healing journey. But the reality of it is, without my own digging and my own work towards healing, I could not heal and could not grow. In the same way that trees in a forest are all connected down in the earth through their roots, those alongside us are there as supports and to help warn us. But they cannot do the work for us. If you enjoy nature at all, I encourage you to read the book *The Hidden Life of Trees*, by Peter Wohlleben. Nature has so much to teach us. Trees don't grow for one another; they support one another in their growth. This is all another human being can do for you as well. No one is coming to heal you—you have that healing power inside you already, you just need to tap into it. And it's okay, even wise, to ask for help in the process.

Many people say that things happen for a reason in life. I challenge this statement. I disagree. I don't believe that my abuse was supposed to happen to me. I don't believe anyone's abuse is supposed to happen. I don't believe slavery was supposed to happen, I don't believe Native Americans were supposed to be slaughtered for the sake of European immigrants, I don't believe that white supremacy should exist, I don't believe we should turn our eye to how black and brown Americans have been treated for years and years, I don't believe segregation should have happened, or should still be happening today in any form. I don't believe that the earth should be treated as it is, or that climate change should be happening. I don't believe it. It's our own human fault that these things have happened—because we decided to play God. We decided we knew right from wrong, who was better than who, who deserved what, and who should have power over another. None of this was what was meant for us or life itself.

The vibrations of love that are to be formed on this earth were never meant to be corrupted by the human ideas that came about because we thought we could play the role of the one who created love itself. We not only have destroyed the earth, but we have destroyed one another. The earth is crying out, desperate to be healed, right alongside so many humans. Just like humans want to be saved, the earth is wanting humans to stand up and remember who they are and get back to the vibration of love energy they came to the earth to experience. The earth wants us to remember the spirits we were before we decided to come into our mothers' wombs. Each and every object, blade of grass, animal, tree, insect, sound, drop of water, all of it, is connected to the same source of love. Ignorantly, arrogantly, we think we can control it, we think we can decide what order it all goes in, forgetting that we should give sovereignty to the very vibrations coming out of each, and praise to the very source it all comes from.

This is where religion gets it wrong: the rigid structure, the dogmatic demands, the call to focus on one group over another. We forget to look at how nature teaches us that it all works together, that we are all interdependent. Instead, the hierarchical systems focus on sex, gender, political agreements and disagreements, supporting and not supporting certain people or topics, deciding who is above, who is below, and who can teach what, forgetting that learning cannot be forced or controlled, but arises from the Divine source itself. Even a child or baby has more wisdom at times than an adult due to their innocent and open connection to their creator, not yet programmed by the lines and limitations the egoic world has created, still living in connection to the spirit world. They have not been tainted and taught how to stay in the lines and think as adults think. We can learn from nature and children if we just sit and watch and listen.

Everyone is worthy in this world. We just don't all know it or remember it. We need guidance, maybe a little push or prodding forward, reminding, just as I am hoping to do as you read these words. But we are not meant to be formed into the mold of what others believe we should be. We are not meant to be placed in a line to blindly follow another—not even our parents, our religion, our schools, or the erroneous beliefs we develop about ourselves; no one, not our best friend, not our spouse, not our teachers, not our government—only we (our inner, higher selves), know our true calling. And to get to that, we need to get out of the line, take a risk, and go inward. Trust me that when you do decide to get out of the line, it may be scary, but it will be liberating and freeing.

Getting out of the line is scary. You truly never know what is ahead. There may be a wreck, there may be a stalled car, there may be an unexpected detour, or just a moment of pause, but we never know unless we try. But the try is worth it. I believe that the universe finally gave me a little push into the unknown, to get out of the line of religion, and step into my healing. I didn't expect it. The day I noticed the traffic backed up, and the pattern of human behavior that was vividly portrayed there, was the day that began to change my thinking. I started to be aware. I started to watch things more closely. I noticed patterns. I saw how easily we fall into line and follow one another without question.

Not that we shouldn't have mentors or people we trust and ask for help. I fully believe that there are people divinely put into our lives for that purpose. I have had many. I believe some of my school-teachers I had growing up were those people. I believe some of my friends have been those people. I believe that I have had some bosses who were teachers for me. I also believe that my therapist is one of those people. All these people showed up and mentored me, prodded me, and taught me. Yet it is I that has had to walk the path. All of these people can support me, cheer me on, offer perspective, and guide me as I walk my path, but the reality is I alone must walk it.

I also have come to understand that I may pass some of them along the way. Just because they are my teacher or mentor for a season, does not mean I have to stay underneath them for a lifetime. The best teachers know that their job is to make the student better, to push them forward in life, to give them everything they can and let them grow beyond, maybe (and hopefully) even to become someone greater than themselves. If you meet people like this in your life, those who want to push you forward and see you succeed, even to the point of watching you do greater things in the world than themselves, hold on to these people, these are true jewels in life. These are the people who have done the inner work and understand that it isn't a competition to get to the top. It is about serving and supporting one another in our individual calling, because the success of one benefits us all.

I had a professor in college that would always speak the kindest words to me. At this time I had no self-worth, had not done any healing, and I had no idea what she saw in me. It was like a foreign language she spoke over me. But she encouraged me. She saw my potential. She always told me she saw great things in me and that I would do great things in life. I didn't believe it back then. I always had a small mindset. Later, when I would do something that felt significant, I would think of her and think maybe that was what she meant. But as I have grown in my awakening process, I have begun to see what she saw all along. She saw strength, someone healed, someone who was able to take all the traumas of the past, the ones she didn't even know I had experienced, and use them for good. She saw me truly, even when I didn't see myself. These are the people you must find in life. If you don't have these people, find them. Seek them out. These are the people that will cheer you on when you speak out your dreams that sound crazy to everyone else. These are the people that will help you open doors when you see a vision of doing something big in the world. These are the people that won't limit you. They are the trees beside you that reach their roots out, hold on under the dirt of life, and help nurse you back to health when you feel defeated, even when you maybe didn't realize they were doing it, and then watch you grow bigger than themselves and they are proud of you. These are your people!

Several of my therapists have been teachers for me. What I found in my healing journey was that as I healed, I needed to find a therapist that understood where I was in my healing journey. I went through three different therapists in a four year period. This is something I want to help people understand. You do not have to sign a life contract to a therapist. Do not feel as if you are committed to someone if they are no longer serving you and helping you. As I said before, you grow and learn, and sometimes what their skill level gave you is what you needed at the time and they were meant to be there for a season in

your life as a helper and healer for you. I think
sometimes we get stuck in a season and are afraid to
move forward because of fear of hurting others. I
know I have been this way. I am a very loyal person.
I hate hurting people and so I find myself sticking
around for others way longer than I probably should.
Even friends who have hurt me, I have given far too
many chances. I think it is okay to try to allow for
others' faults and to love them and give second
chances. But when it starts to hinder your progress in
life, and keep you from your calling and growth, that
is when you need to understand that it is okay to let
people go. Just like the trees, it is okay to grow. The
trees don't stay small because another tree isn't
growing. It grows, knowing that if it grows, it will help
grow a forest, and slowly, the others will come up
behind it. It is not a competition; it is a beautiful
creation. It is not that you are better than another, or
someone else is better than you, it just means we all
have different seasons, different lessons, and
different things to teach and learn from one another.
Just as if the earth has a different orbit and the light
hits each side a different time, and the seasons hit at
different times in different places, we need to allow
that to happen in each other's lives as well. Maybe
your growth will inspire your friend to grow. Maybe
your friend moving on will inspire you to grow. You
never know what can happen when you decide to

choose you and stop living small for the sake of
others.

I truly believe that as you grow, alignment will
happen. Those meant to be on your journey will align
with you. In a prior chapter I mentioned my best
friend that I met in college. We spent many years out
of alignment. We did not always speak the same
language. Over the years we both grew on our own
spiritual paths and in our own ways. We never lived
near each other after that first year of college, and so
it is unique for us to have remained best friends for
this long. To have such a friend that loves and
supports you in the good and bad times is a precious
thing. As we have both grown, it has been beautiful
to watch our lives align. We never were able to speak
to each other as authentically as we have recently. I
believe in my awakening process I was able to come
to a place I didn't fear being myself, and she had
been in her own process in life of showing up as her
true authentic self as well. With two people being
able to show up as themselves in a friendship and
relationship, there is no fear. There are opportunities
for both of us to feel safe to share our feelings
openly. That means, if I am in a bad mood, or if she
says something that makes me mad, I tell her. I don't
fear losing the friendship because of this. I don't fear
her ignoring me, not responding to a text message

the next day, or not talking to me for months after this. I know that she will respond when she is ready if I upset her. But I don't fear the lack of relationship because I know the relationship is built on a firm foundation of trust. This is rare. I couldn't be more thankful for this friendship and the time it took to develop it.

At one point I really did think we might not ever be as close as we are now. Because of our growing experiences taking us on very different paths many different times in life, we had moments of silence in our friendship. When we began to align again, I realized something. When you trust the universe, God, your higher self, the source of Love to lead and guide you in all things and to heal you, things always align the way they are supposed to. So just because something doesn't seem as if it is aligned in the moment, doesn't mean it won't be down the road. Time is a human interpretation, not an energetic or spiritual one. Once we are out of these human bodies, none of us will have a concept of time. No worries, no rush, no need to control. We will just be. I am, that I am. So, if something doesn't seem to be aligning at this point, something that you feel energetically should be in your life, maybe it means you just need to rest, adjust your energy, refocus on yourself, and that will realign the thing you are currently worried about. You cannot control another human no matter how much you want to.

I remember how hard it was when I started to choose myself. I felt panic over it. I didn't want to tell people no, ever! I always showed up. I was the one people could count on. Slowly, I began to burn out, and stopped being able to show up because I just couldn't. When I started to heal and I moved into my spiritual awakening more and more, the therapist I had at the time no longer seemed to meet my needs. She was the most wonderful lady and I adored her. She was the therapist that had helped me on my healing journey the most up until that point. It was when Covid hit that things changed, and then my dad passed. We had to change to video therapy, which was hard, especially having so many significant events happening in my life at once. This therapist was from a Christian office and I had picked her because at the time I still thought myself to be a Christian. She wasn't like most of the Christians I had talked to or been around and was more aligned with my understanding than others, so I felt more comfortable talking to her about some of my awakening that was happening, but not all of it. I still held back on some of the things happening to me for fear of judgment.

It was in September 2020, that things switched. I was fired from my job on September 18th, which was devastating, as I loved my job and was trying my best to manage it on top of all the other things going on in my life with my dad's cancer, a foster daughter at home, and COVID having just begun shortly before. Five very short days later, my dad passed away, and then just a day after the funeral, which wasn't much of a funeral because of COVID, my foster daughter became dysregulated in my home, throwing things at me, telling me she hated me and wanted to leave. She was 18, and there was nothing I could do to stop her. I had planned to adopt her and I didn't have anything else in me at that point to fight against this. I had hit my breaking point, and had nothing in me to give her what she needed in that moment. I know now that it likely was because of all the traumatic events I was going through that she became so dysregulated and was unable to handle the events just as much as myself. I was so unstable at the time, no wonder she felt unstable. I let her go that day. This left me with three major losses at once. My heart was completely broken.

That same day, I put a bag in my car and drove ten hours to the state next to mine to the mountains and hiked for two weeks, staying in hotels where I could find them. I was in complete shock and in a dissociative state. Because of all of this happening at once, I had tremendous grief to work through and I had become numb. Not only was I trying to work through all my old trauma, I was now dealing with all of this current loss too. My hiking trip to the mountains sustained my strength for a while, and I felt liberated by it. Going on a solo hiking trip gave me a sense of being strong and able to make it through all this alone. But the reality was I wasn't that strong. I needed help. I was already in therapy, but COVID had become such a part of our daily lives that we all were living in isolation. I was bound to my home, seeing no one in person for months. I spent my days looking for jobs, applying for over ten a day, trying to make it through interviews without crying, and I worked with my therapist over video. I spent most days crawling up on my couch crying, and remembering the night my dad passed away trying to burn the image of his face out of my mind somehow by thinking of other things. I would go hiking every day that the weather would allow me to, and I would sometimes facetime friends that were in touch with me at the time. Yet, no one knew how painful all of this was for me. Because of all the trauma in my life, I had learned to show up as strong and remain silent about how much I was hurting. Only one of my friends tried to open up to me. But slowly, she also pulled away, and before I knew it, I found myself completely alone during a pandemic, and only doing video therapy.

I was able to find a new job after three months. It was something I wasn't familiar with but I was able to adjust. My boss was states away, which made it more challenging, but I pushed through. I spent my days quietly at home. I didn't turn my TV on, as I knew that filling my mind with more sadness about the pandemic and watching things that made me feel bad would just cause more grief. My friends were losing family members, I was watching people on social media lose people, and I just couldn't handle it. I spend my days and nights allowing myself to cry as much as I needed to. Sometimes yelling and screaming as well. But I knew I needed to get through the pain somehow. I began to understand that feeling my pain was crucial, that it was in the feeling that I would heal. So, I went inward.

I started to meditate every day. I started out with just three minutes, then five minutes, then ten, and before I knew it, I was meditating for an hour or more. I started to notice a change in myself. I realized it was working. It was helping me heal. Then I noticed each time I would meet with my therapist over video, I wasn't resonating with the things she was telling me to do to heal. Over the next few months I would talk to her about how I didn't know what I believed about Heaven or Hell, or God, or Jesus, or anything I once believed. She would quote bible verses to me as she tried to encourage me in my Christian faith and help me get back on track. I am thankful she tried, I really am. But I was no longer the same, something had changed, and I think she knew as well. She began to schedule me out one month at a time, and slowly I felt more and more lost.

My close friends started to disconnect from me at this time as well—each of us going through our own challenges, needing to take space to reassess and find our way. This caused me to feel even more alone. I decided it was time to move on to a new therapist. I looked online for about a month. I wanted to continue doing EMDR which had been helpful, so I needed someone with that training. Not finding anyone in my current town, I had to look elsewhere. I didn't just want anyone, I needed someone I felt I could trust, someone who would actually help me heal. Having worked in mental health myself, I have always had a hard time connecting with a therapist who I didn't feel like was just going through the motions with me. I wanted someone real. I found a website that struck me. I kept returning to it over and over and re-read it several times before I decided to pull the trigger and email this person. I am so glad I did. It ended up being one of the best decisions so far in my healing journey.

I had noticed on her website she listed hypnotherapy as a process she engaged in with her clients. Because of my spiritual awakening, I was intrigued. Before my awakening I would never have done this. In one way, I wonder if I contacted her because I was being rebellious. I wrote my current therapist to let her know I had found someone new— it was a nice letter thanking her for all of her help, and for pushing me forward in my healing.

It occurred to me that my spiritual awakening was taking a new turn. I was going to begin to open up to gifts in my life that I had ignored, experience things from my childhood that I had forgotten, and uncover hidden parts of me that both trauma and religion had convinced me were negative.

I bring this experience up about changing therapists to demonstrate again that your healing journey is in your own hands. It is not up to anyone else to heal you. You are fully capable of taking your life in the direction you need, to find the help you need for your healing. Keep in mind, even the best therapist can't heal you. But they can sure help! I also want to encourage you to find someone who has done their own healing. A healer must have also been on a healing journey themselves. It is hard to help others heal if you have not done the hard work yourself. Most people are able to lead others because they have taken the journey and are familiar with the terrain. They don't need to have had the same experiences, but having someone who understands that healing isn't always easy or comfortable, someone who clearly has made it through to become whole again, will help give you confidence to push through in moments when you get uncomfortable yourself. There may be times you want to give up or feel tired of it all, so having someone who helps push you through those moments is important. Someone who can look at you and believe you are worth the healing. I was and am thankful to have found that. And that is what I inspire myself to do for others. I believe your life will continue to repeat the same cycles until you dare to walk into your own healing. Lessons tend to come over and over until you learn from them, or until they push you to the point of having to look at yourself in the mirror, to really look at yourself and decide it is time to heal because you no longer want to live in the cycle of pain, or stay stuck and small in life.

In the summer of 2004 I had a very vivid vision. The vision about the leaf this book is about. As I was waking up one morning, still half asleep, I began to see a leaf. It was dead, brown, crusted up, as if it had just detached from an autumn tree, the last one to fall, and was about to hit the ground for the winter, never to be seen again. I watched the leaf fall from the sky and into a stream. In the vision, my vantage point was up in the sky, as if I was among the stars, looking down. As I looked down at the stream I could see the entire scene very clearly. The stream began as a natural spring, bubbling up from the earth, so clear and beautiful that you could see to the bottom as it pooled and flowed. There were a multitude of colored rocks at the bottom of it. The pool itself was only deep enough that the leaf could float above the crystal clear water, the rocks below almost like crystals. The water glistened under the sunlight, and there were huge, beautifully green, luscious trees that lined the stream. It was as if the stream was its own trail within the forest and no one knew about it but its own self, unseen and untouched by any human. It was immeasurably radiant as though nothing had ever touched it. Pure, unpolluted. I watched this dead leaf begin to float with the current down the stream. I noticed that down the stream there were some large rocks sticking up, more ordinary gray in color, like normal stream rocks I would see on an everyday occasion.

I watched the leaf flow with the stream gently, unhindered, until it got stuck behind the first large gray rock. As I watched, I noticed the leaf appeared to be frantically trying to move around the rock. It was hitting up against the rock, banging it, almost as if it was panicking and stressing about being stuck behind it knowing that it needed to get around it to get where it wanted to be. Watching from above I could see that if the leaf would just rest, the flow of the stream would take it around the rock. But because the leaf was fighting, it was causing itself to be stuck. I wanted to yell down and tell it to stop fighting the current, or reach my hand down and stop it from fighting, but for some reason I knew that I needed to allow it to fight against the rock. I watched in agony wanting so badly to help. But all I could do was hope it would calm down and let the stream help it around. After a while, which seemed to be a long while, it became tired, slowly stopped fighting, and began to rest. Once it had stopped and rested completely, the stream picked it up in its current like a loving parent or friend, and carried it on its way. I watched this process happen a few more times behind other big rocks, and each time it was just as painful to watch as it was the first time—the struggle of the leaf trying to fight against the rock and get around it.

The more I watched, I noticed something beautiful happening. It appeared that the leaf would get a bit quicker at calming down. Then I noticed around the fourth rock that the color of the leaf was changing. It was no longer brown, but was changing from brown to orange to yellow to gold, all the colors of fall, but as if it was going backwards. I was amazed. Then it dawned on me: the leaf was coming back to life! Each time it would make it around a rock, it would gain more color and continue on its journey in a more colorful and powerful way. As the leaf's journey continued, it became more and more agile at getting around the rocks, learning to rest, trusting the current to carry it, until it came to the point where it would get stuck, notice it was stuck, and just rest there until it moved around, not reacting or responding to the difficulty of the rock in its way. It just knew the stream would take it around, and all it needed to do was rest, wait, and trust the divine flow of the water.

As the leaf passed what appeared to be the last large rock in the stream, I saw that the stream ended in a beautiful waterfall. I couldn't see where the waterfall went from my point of view, but I noticed the leaf was completely green and full of life by this time. As it fell off the waterfall, it floated into the sky taken by the wind, leaving the earth with no worry or concern, knowing that it was healed and full of life.

Then I heard a voice. "This is you. You are the leaf." Immediately I saw a vision of myself full of energy and light, laying my hands on people and healing them.

I woke from this vision in a daze and almost in shock.

As you can tell, I have never forgotten this vision. It will forever be imprinted in my mind. It was a clear message of healing for me, and a message of hope. I also don't believe it was just a message for me, but a message I was to share with the world. The leaf isn't just about my healing, but the healing of you. The healing of those who are ready to trust the journey and the lessons in life, to learn from the leaf lessons.

The part where I was laying my hands on people and healing them confused me for a long time. The church I had been part of taught about laying on of hands and healing people—all for the purpose of bringing friends and family to the knowledge of Jesus as their savior. So I had thought that was what that vision meant: that I was going to heal many people in the church. I now understand it to be something completely different.

After my awakening, and after my dad passed away in September 2020, I started to meditate daily. At first I could only do it for about five minutes at a time as I was so distracted, and I could barely make it sitting even that long. So I started to meditate several times a day to see if I could increase my time and learn to focus more. I don't know what provoked me to do so, but something in me desired to expand my study of things outside my religion. I had already been studying Buddhism for a few years after discovering it on trips I had taken to Southeast Asia. I had started learning more about the energy of crystals, and I had heard about things such as psychics and tarot cards. But I only knew of these things on a surface level. So I started to study them more seriously. I also started looking deeper into astrology, learning more about my sun, moon, and rising signs and learning about my friends' signs so I could understand them more. I began searching for mentors and people who had also had spiritual awakenings, because I was feeling very alone in my experience. I began to see there was much more to the world than the small box I had been living in. All the fear I had been taught by religion to have toward these other things started to fade away, and I began to be intrigued instead. In my meditations I was starting to experience new things and to find healing in ways I didn't expect. I knew something important was shifting for me.

I also learned about energy healing. I began to see references to this thing called "energy healing" all over the place and wondered if it was something I was supposed to look into. I studied and became a Reiki practitioner and then remembered the part of my dream about placing my hands on people and helping them. I was coming to understand that my vision was preparing me to be a healer. All those years ago, it was telling me that as I trusted the process of healing for myself, I would move into the calling of my own life. Since this time, I have also worked on getting my Mindfulness Certification and Life Coach Certification.

Even though I do not believe that all things, especially traumas, happen for a reason, I do believe that anything can be used for good. It does not mean that the thing that happened to us was a good thing, it just means that we can choose to use it for the good of ourselves and others. We can allow the vibrations of love to enter our wounds and heal them in order to allow those scars to then help others heal. Because humans have tried to put themselves in the place of God since the beginning, causing unnecessary harm to ourselves and other living beings on the planet, we have had to figure out how to help one another heal. We have not always done a very good job at that. But there always have been and continue to be souls on this earth who get it. I have met a few of them. They are beautiful light workers who I feel privileged to know and to have known. I am sure I will get to meet many more on my journey.

The lesson of the leaf in my vision showed me that it is in trusting our own journey, accepting ourselves and the position we find ourselves in, that we learn the process of healing. No other leaf was able to move that leaf around the rocks. I myself wasn't able to reach out and move that leaf around the rock. The leaf itself had to learn the lesson of trusting the journey, the divine current of the stream, and allow itself to relax and rest. The more it learned, the easier it got. Each of us have to learn to trust that stream to carry us around the rocks we get stuck behind. Some of us farther along the journey can help teach the other leaves, encourage them along the way, inspire them to trust and let go a little more, but we can't stay stuck behind the rock ourselves for the purpose of helping another leaf make it around or all we are doing is causing yet another traffic jam, blocking the flow, and losing faith in the very same flow we are trying to encourage others to trust.

Another lesson of the leaf is that as we trust the journey of the stream, we must continue to leave previous parts of the stream behind. Sometimes it is hard to leave things behind. We might actually have enjoyed our time behind the rock. Sometimes our struggles, though painful, offer the comfort of familiarity—of being what we have always known. As weird as that might sound, having the struggle could have fulfilled something inside of us that we didn't realize it did. Having the struggle allowed us to have something to focus on, or to get attention from the rock, or to be with the other leaves that were stuck behind the rock. Maybe we became friends with other leaves, and struggled alongside them, and were afraid to leave them behind. Eventually we may see one of our leaf friends find their own calm, and slide on to continue their journey, and we might become jealous or envious of their progress. I think it might even be possible to never leave that rock and make a home there, living an entire life never fully blooming into what you were made to be on the earth, yet the whole time watching other leaves move along and feeling justified to be angry about it because you know where they came from and now they are teaching other leaves how to get around the rock. Yet, there you are, still behind it. Still gathered there with the other leaves, piled up, and making your home, refusing to rest in the stream that can take you along the same path as the friend that moved on to the next phase of the stream.

There are so many lessons within the leaf lesson. So many ways to see this small yet mighty vision. It is why I share the hard lessons of my story, and open up about things I have never opened up about to anyone other than my therapist. I hope in doing so to shed light on the world, and to help some leaves find their value and understand that they do not have to stay stuck behind the rocks of life. There are those of us who have been there and were able to get around them. It is not that we have conquered life and know all the answers. We are still facing rocks, and will be until we get to the end of this life cycle. It is, however, possible to trust the journey, learn from our lessons, to lay back and trust the current of the stream, to trust the universe to guide us to our next season.

Just lay back and rest like a leaf in a stream, trust your journey of healing, allow the rocks of life to teach you the lessons they are there to teach you, but don't allow yourself to stay stuck behind them any longer than necessary. There is too much beauty ahead to stay stuck behind a stagnant gray rock.

The Point of Forgiveness

Most of us who have spent time in any church setting have heard a lot about judgment. The first is about God's judgment upon humans. The second is about judging one another. I always found it interesting how much we could focus on how God would judge us and all of our behaviors, and how that justified us being able to judge one another and each other's behaviors. Somehow, we decided we could stand in God's place, judge others as sinners, and threaten them with going to hell. Of course only certain behaviors are seen as sins, and where the line gets drawn is different depending on individual interpretation.

White lies seem to be okay, if they are protecting someone, while an outright lie isn't usually acceptable. The lies that we tell once in a while to make sure we don't hurt one another are fine. Or the ones to keep someone from knowing something that might cause something to get out about something we know that we learned through gossip—those are ok. Which—gossip—is okay in some circumstances as it allows us to ask for prayer for other people's sins. "Did you hear that Sue and David had sex this weekend? And they aren't married! They need prayer." The next thing you know, that person is telling someone else, "I feel like maybe I should tell you just for the purpose of praying for them, that Sue and David are having sex outside of marriage. They really need prayer to make the right choices and keep themselves pure." This could go on and on.

What I always found frustrating about these situations is that what could actually help this person from the start would be to go to them directly and ask if they even want prayer or support for this, and if so, what kind? What would help would be to be honest and genuine, tell them what you had heard, let them know that it is really none of your business if it is true or not, but if they need support with anything you are there for them. Who knows? Maybe the rumor or gossip being spread isn't even true. I myself have been caught up in this. I believed I was doing 'good' by sharing the information I had found out with someone else for the purpose of prayer. It was how I was programmed to think. But really, what I have come to understand is that it is no one's business. And if I really do care about that person, I need to go to them directly and talk to them face to face. If I have a relationship with them that is trusting, then I can offer my support. If I don't, then I need to stay out of it. I especially should keep my judgments out of it. When someone knows they are not going to be judged for their choices, decisions, behaviors, or even mistakes, they are more likely to approach someone for help or support.

We also tend to label sins from good to bad. Some are okay, others worse, and some are unforgivable. I remember conversations with others after someone had died. People would say things like, "They weren't walking with the Lord when they died," or, "They were homosexual," or, "They drank a lot" or, "They never accepted the Lord as their savior," or, "They wandered from the church, I just don't know if they made it to heaven." When I heard such things it always made me feel uneasy, as if they were taking some kind of pleasure in knowing the person did not make it to heaven, or in knowing a secret others didn't, or that the other person's failures made them feel better about their own.

This always made me sad. In my awakening process I would sometimes tell others about God's grace and love, explaining that I could still call out to God to receive this love and grace no matter what, only to be shut down very quickly with comments about God's judgment. I don't believe people do this out of hate or because they are hopeful people go to a place called hell. I think it is just a part of the conditioning of the mind, a part of one of the lines that has been formed in religious thinking over thousands of years. Through this kind of conditioning we forget our true selves, our innate wisdom, and cave in to believing what other humans have taught us, thinking that they know the truth and maybe we don't.

In my awakening process I have come to the belief that deep down, we all know the truth. It is deeply planted inside of us, even if buried beneath mountains of conditioning. We are programmed and conform to lines that are taught through religion. In this process, we are taught to emphasize some sins more than others. For example, in the church I was a part of, we didn't talk a lot about things such as envy, gluttony, greed, pride, or sloth. There wasn't as much focus on venial sins, which are sins that are seen as forgivable while some of the others are not. There was a lot of focus on being born sinners in general and needing to be saved by being accepted by Jesus, and his blood covering our sins. But there wasn't much attention paid to loving the unlovable. It seemed instead that Jesus' purpose on earth was to come and die for us so that we can live and go to heaven. Unless we believe and confess that he is our savior and did this for us we are unable to go there ourselves. The focus in most of the sermons I attended was on the prerequisites for being a saved human to go to heaven. One may argue with that assessment, I know in the past I would have become very defensive if I heard that. I would have even argued with someone who had said this. Pride has a way of making us blind to our own selves. We even become blind to our own pride. Having experienced both sides, being on the inside of religion, and now on the outside of it, I understand it from both perspectives. I am thankful for that now, as I can relate and help educate from both sides.

Being awakened spiritually, I see and understand how one can become both defensive to such things and yet blind to judgment. In my awakening I came to understand that I was not just walking in religion but pride. I had taken on a form of

127

hate in my heart. Believing I was better than others because I had figured things out that they had not. I even remember having thoughts about loved ones who had died not making it to heaven. It made me sad, but I really allowed my heart to accept that they were burning in an eternal fire in hell because they did not accept Jesus as their savior. Of course, I didn't know for sure, but based on their lifestyle, and things I had been taught, this was my belief. I truly felt sad about this and wished it weren't true, but nothing outside of my own understanding at that time could tell me differently. The book I was reading and the teachings I was under all told me this to be true and the line I was standing in confirmed this thinking, so at the time, it was my truth. I knew that there was a certain way of doing things and if you did not do it that way, eternal judgment had to happen.

It was not until my awakening in 2016 that I came to understand that all of my thinking was based on pride and my own ego. Religion was created by man trying to figure out God, and in the process almost putting himself in the place of God, trying to control other human beings. This kind of religion creates fear, fear of damnation, punishment, permanent pain and suffering. And fear makes people easy to control. The sins were determined— some of them quite sensible, others more culturally

or politically motivated—and at various times some
sins were deemed worse than others. In my
exploration of the bible, after reading it many times
over, I always wondered about the thorn in Paul's
side. I myself tried to relate it to my own sins, and
things I personally struggled with. I tended to relate
the things I read to experiences in my own life. I had
a suspicion the thorn in Paul's side had something
sexual about it, and I began to wonder if Paul might
have been homosexual—something the people of his
time might have judged him harshly for. I am unsure
what the thoughts on homosexuality were at that time
period. Homosexuality was not originally considered
a sin in the bible—it was named as such by someone
later in the church. At some point along the line there
was a need to define it as a sin and to degrade
anyone who was involved in a same sex relationship.
I'm not saying I am completely right in what I am
saying about this text or about Paul. But these are
conclusions I have come to understand in my own
study of how the bible was developed and edited
over the centuries. I do know that over time there
seemed to be a shifting hierarchy of sins, some being
worse than others for a time, and then others
becoming more serious and so on. I myself believed
some to be worse than others.

I have formed a list below and I would like to see if any of you have experienced the same things I have in this regard. On the list below, I am going to name ten sins. I invite you to number them 1 through 10, putting a 1 beside the worst sin and going on up to the 10 beside the least. For example, if you think smoking is the worst sin you could ever commit, put a number 1 beside that, if you think gluttony (eating too much) is the least sin, put a 10 by that. Fill in each sin according to what you believe.

Least to Worst Sins

1 through 10

_____overeating

_____sex outside of marriage

_____smoking (cigarettes)

_____drugs (any kind)

_____looking at someone with lust

_____masturbation

_____gossip

_____stealing

_____lying

_____homosexuality

What was the worst sin you listed?

What was the least sin you listed?

Why did you choose the worst sin?

Why did you choose the least sin?

Did you pick your least to worst sins? Did it take you very long to pick them? What helped guide you to pick these sins? Things you heard in church? Things you heard from friends? Things you read in the bible? Bible studies? Maybe your parents taught this? What was behind the choice?

Now that you are thinking about these questions, let's also think about this. Did you ever stop to think about the fact that you labeled sins? That you were trained to think that way? That somehow, as in the prior chapter we talked about, you got in that line and didn't realize you were in it? That you have been programmed to think a certain way without any awareness you were taught to think it? I never once thought about this until I had my spiritual awakening. Not once did I step back to consider that every single event in my life programmed me to think a certain way. I could argue my point fully believing that I was right and someone else was wrong just because I was taught to believe something. There are, of course, absolute truths in the world. Things such as science and love are two of them. But even science and earthly love fall short.

I fully confess to you that had I read this book before my awakening I 1000% would have labeled those sins believing I was absolutely right in knowing that some were worse than others, and having excuses for my own behaviors. I will even admit to how I would have labeled them because there is still an uncontrolled ego inside of me that sometimes pops its dirty head up believing it can control my spirit. Just so you know that you are not alone. I 100% would have said either sex outside of marriage or homosexuality was one of the worst sins. Then, moving down to drugs, masturbation, smoking, lying and then down to the not so bad sins that we occasionally do because we are human of course, the overeating and lust, and gossip, of course, which sometimes happens because of prayer requests.

It really is amazing how one can justify one's own behaviors as not so bad, and yet look at another's behaviors and believe they are so much worse. There is even a scientific term for this tendency, called the *fundamental attribution error*. We see our own behaviors as not so bad because we are aware of all the factors contributing to our decision to act that way (things we could not control), whereas we see the other's behavior as purely arising out of their own flawed character or moral delinquency.

I remember sitting and arguing with friends about certain situations or behaviors, convinced of my opinions about other people. Now I think back to those times with shame and remorse about my attitude, recognizing the pride I had in my heart to think I was completely right and they were wrong. I regret how I must have made them feel. Knowing what I know now, how my programming taught me the beliefs I had, and how my trauma on top of all that led me to want to find something to hold onto that kept me safe, I forgive myself for not knowing any better. I give myself grace. At times it's hard and I have to remind myself to be kind to myself, to that part of me that is still deconstructing out of the programmed mindset and into the understanding of my higher self. I am thankful that it is so very true that when you continue to seek for what you desire you eventually find it. I am just amazed that I did not find what I thought I was going to find. None of this is what I thought I would find.

This leads me to yet another experience and vision I had. This vision was during a meditative state, in which my dad came to visit me, and I was able to hear him speaking to me. I am so very thankful that God has led people into my life who have helped me understand some of these experiences I have had. In my previously programmed mind I would have had much fear about them. I can't say enough about the importance of surrounding yourself with people aligned with your highest purpose and energy. I would be lost without the people who truly understood what I was talking about when I talked about woo-woo things. Having someone you feel safe with is important.

Though my dad had passed away in September of 2020 from cancer, I still was processing some of my experiences with him throughout my life and feeling the loss of not having him in my life as a father figure. I didn't have a ton of interactions with him growing up because my parents divorced when I was very young, but the interactions I had with him were not always the most pleasant memories. No one would likely have known they were not pleasant as I did not tell anyone about these feelings or experiences.

Growing up I often felt invisible. I remember being in a room with my dad and feeling completely unseen. I don't know that he ever did it on purpose, but it was how I felt. I can point out specific times in my life standing beside him, or being around him and feeling completely ignored or unseen. Having only a "Hi, Ang," from him, and nothing else. I always felt like the invisible one in the family, especially around him. Knowing more about my trauma growing up and things I experienced and how they formed my thinking, as well as how I blocked out many memories through dissociation, I understand some of why I felt that way. But I do know for sure there were moments that this did happen. My dad in his spirit has confirmed this to me, and in his pure, healed self, has asked me to forgive him. I am thankful he has come to me and helped me to understand that it is okay to allow myself to have felt these things. I believe sometimes we unconsciously deal with our traumas by assuming we made up those disturbing images or memories. This leads us to hold them in our bodies and start to form beliefs around these situations and about ourselves to make sense of them. These unprocessed traumas can then manifest into physical symptoms as well. For a long time I believed I needed to stay invisible, that I needed to stay small in the world. I also had formed a belief that although I had a lot of good potential, I would never fully reach it because I wasn't good enough to do so.

Throughout most of my childhood and into my teens and early adulthood, I had to protect myself by shutting off most of my thoughts and feelings so I could show up in the world. I had to escape from my feelings, emotions, and mind in order to survive some of the things I experienced. I did not understand until later in life that this is called dissociation. I also did not know I was experiencing it myself until I was well into my therapy process in my forties. One day my therapist pointed out to me that I had a lot of dissociative moments. I had no clue. Having worked in mental health for many years I had seen it in clients, I could recognize it in them, but I hadn't seen it in myself. After my therapist pointed this out, I looked back at my own experiences and recognized some of the signs: time would pass and I would not remember it passing, or huge blocks in my life I did not remember, or moments in time I could not recall. I also had moments I would zone out and not hear what people said to me, or when I had a hard time processing information. I remember at times people would say things to me and I would stare at them blankly and not know how to respond. I now know it was because I was dissociated, not fully present when they were talking, so I really did not even hear them. I was too embarrassed to ask them to repeat what they said because I was sure they would think I was stupid or incapable.

I remember this happening with a supervisor one time. It was a hard moment for me, as this was a turning point in our relationship that ended up causing a very positive relationship to turn sour. She had said something to me and I was already in a triggered state, and I remember sitting there just looking at her. I honestly was just processing what she said and had no idea what to say back. I don't even know if I knew what she said to me. She became upset and stormed out of my office. I remember feeling so defeated in that moment, and going straight back to my invisible state, the same feelings I always had when I felt unseen by my dad. It was then I started to feel that same way around her. Sadly this relationship never recovered, and even now I am unable to speak to this person to share with them my understanding about why situations like this happened. However, I do understand more now and I give myself grace for these moments I had. And I understand that having grace for other people's trauma is important too. Maybe she had moments in her life that made her feel unseen and unheard as well, and my state may have caused her to react in the way she did, which allows me to feel grace, love, and forgiveness towards her even now in these memories. I can send light and love to that moment knowing we were both doing the best we could at the time with what we had going on in our lives.

When I got my first job working in mental health with kids I remember reading some of their charts and thinking how much their stories seemed similar to my own. Some of them were mild cases of kids struggling to make good decisions, or to follow rules in school, and needing some guidance on how to calm their body and mind down; some might need ADHD meds, or help with listening. And then there were the harder to hear cases of severe abuse in the home.

Sometimes reading through a chart, it would hit me in the gut that I, too, had been abused. Up to that point I had just assumed my life was like everyone else's—normal. But discovering that many of these children were being referred to our services because of sexual abuse, mental abuse, physical abuse, neglect, divorced parents, and so on, I began to consider my own experiences in a new light. There were things I never considered abuse that were now coming across my desk clearly labeled as abuse. I was shocked. I had completely shut my awareness off to the actual nature of my experiences—I never even knew that this was not normal.

I had many other friends who had divorced parents, and I could easily relate with them. We didn't talk about it of course, but it was understood. I also never really shared anything with anyone about my home life. Now that I think about it, I didn't even have friends come and stay the night when we lived with my abusive stepdad—of course. As the years went by in my work with children, I started to understand that I lived with a lot of unprocessed childhood abuse, and I began to have what is called counter transference with my clients. Counter transference is when you begin to have an emotional reaction toward a client, rather than being objective. It is usually because you have had a similar experience as the client or are being triggered by the client in some way. This is common in therapy and in the mental health field and if the person in the helping position is not aware that this is happening it can be very damaging to the therapeutic process for the client. If the person in the helping position is able to recognize this, it does not pose a problem, but the person in the helping position must have done their own healing work to be able to handle these moments with integrity. An unhealed healer that experiences countertransference can begin to behave toward a client in problematic ways and potentially harm their treatment. I am hopeful I never caused harm to any of my clients. However, I do know early on in my career I was unaware of how to separate myself from my clients and their experiences, and sometimes I found myself in tears after an experience with one of them.

I do believe that over time mental health has changed for the better and it has allowed for the helper to be more real with their clients in their healing process, however it is important to keep yourself protected and to do your own healing work if you are working in any kind of healing field. This is something I have had to learn the hard way. Because of my unhealed trauma I spent many years working with clients doing the best I could—I often was given much praise for my work—but I always left exhausted and unable to care for myself at the end of the day. I was not good at self-care, so I began to take on too much in my job and take on the emotions and feelings of my clients. As an empath, I did not protect my own energy. I had no idea how to. Because I cared so deeply about each client and their experiences, I took their problems on myself in attempts to try to help them get through their challenges. This not only did not help the clients I was working with, but it did not help me. I was already carrying so much of my own unprocessed trauma and unhealed energy, that taking on more unhealed energy was detrimental to my mental and physical health. But I wanted to be the best—I wanted to help as many people as I could.

As I began to process the fact that I also had been through trauma and abuse, my heart expanded for those I worked with and I wanted even more to help them. I worked late, working my hardest to be the best at my job, and showed up even when I didn't need to. I stretched myself so thin I began to wear myself out. I had no idea I was actually causing physical harm to my own body. I was gaining more weight, and striving for more solutions in life to be a better person. I always felt defeated. No one would have known that about me. I didn't show up that way when I was out in the world. I naturally hid that part of myself. I remember once a co-worker saying to me that they couldn't figure me out. That statement still sticks with me. I also was told many times that I was intimidating or hard to approach. I always found this to be interesting as I thought of myself as a very kind and loving person. But I also knew I was guarded. I had a full body of armor on and anyone who stepped too close knew it. Not that I would harm them, but I think they would feel the energy shift, the guard going up. It was my fear. It was easier to stay invisible in some areas and seen in others.

Becoming a perfectionist in areas of my life such as work, while hiding the scars of my history, became my game in life. But at home I spent a lot of time crying and striving to get over my pain. I remember spending hours and hours in prayer, reading my bible, begging to be different, to be a better person, friend, coworker. I had no idea that as I was striving and seeking all those years, I was actually manifesting my healing. I was calling out for my healing, but I didn't realize that I wasn't going to get it in the way I was calling out. I thought that somehow Jesus, or God, or some divine intervention would come down one day and suddenly heal me. I would just show up differently in the world one day, a miracle would happen and poof, all my problems would be solved. It never happened. I was broken, worn out and tired. I had no idea how to heal myself, yet I was striving to help others heal on a daily basis.

Then it happened. I came face to face with the fact that I needed to start to heal. Something in me realized that it was time to face all those demons I had hidden deep inside me. It was shortly after my awakening that I started the process of exposing my own trauma. I came face to face with it one day and there was no more denying it.

It was after I had the dream about leaving my church. It was a scary thing for me to do as I had been there for many years. All of my friends were there and leaving this familiar place meant leaving them too. I left my job, then my church, and got a new job very quickly. Then, because I didn't really know what else to do, I started to go to another church on Sunday mornings. I got right back into all the things I had done at my previous church by engaging with the youth group, going to singles events with others my age, and joining bible studies. I was still trying to fit a square peg into a round hole.

My life was changing very quickly around this time, and it almost didn't seem real. I had my new job for only ten months when my dad was diagnosed with cancer. I loved the job, the people I was with, and it was a non-stressful environment. It also allowed me time to be with my dad as he began his cancer treatments. Just that summer we had begun to form a closer relationship with each other.

Then I was contacted by an old friend from the previous job asking if I would like to return. It was a job I loved, and I thought maybe it was my calling. But it didn't fit in the way the new job did. I flip-flopped about what to do, however the old job continued to contact me and ask me to come. I had not yet learned how to say no, or choose myself, so it was hard to turn down, and finally I took it.

I don't regret taking the job. I do believe it was a part of my awakening process and a part of my learning. Had I not taken it I would not have connected with the people I connected with or understood some of the things I understand now. I have a heart of gratitude for the time I had there, and am thankful for the experience. However, the events that took place after this were a hard turn for me. Going back to mental health, dealing with my dad's cancer and the emotions around it, along with my new spiritual awakening was a lot to handle at once. I was feeling a bit strange in the world, alone, with no one to talk to. And then my endometriosis (which had just been diagnosed two years prior) started to flare up and I began to have overwhelming pain in my body.

So all of this was happening as I was starting this new church. Then one day in this new church I suddenly found myself face to face with the very same person who had raped me that night among the broken-down cars. I remember it clearly. It was a strange moment.

There he was—now a man—twenty years older. I had actually seen him once before. I am a photographer and was doing a side business for extra income. That summer I had been hired to do family photos by a realtor team. It was a weekend full of families that came every fifteen minutes to have their family photos taken, so the day moved very quickly, and there was not much time to think in between the sessions. I just posed them and move to the next family. As I got home and began to edit and process the photos, I came across one family and a familiar face popped up. I remember looking at the photo I was about to edit, then the name on the email of who I needed to send the photo to, and I was shocked! It was him. The boy who had raped me in high school. I sat there looking at the photo—of this now man with a wife and two children—thinking, *I wonder if she even has a clue who he is. That he is capable of this. That he did this to another woman.* I felt sick to my stomach that I had to edit this photo and email it to this family. I briefly wondered if he recognized me, or if he remembered what he did to me, but because I needed to get through the editing process, I pushed the thoughts aside, just like I always did, edited the photo and sent the email and moved on to the next family.

I did not expect to see him just months later at the new church I was going to. I remember that day walking into the church, seeing him (with this same woman) looking straight at me, and knowing that he recognized me. In that moment, I knew he remembered what he had done to me. I had a panic attack and left the church. I'm not sure what possessed me to return to the church, maybe I thought it was just a coincidence that he was there that weekend, and that someone who would ever do that to another human would never be in a church setting, but it happened again. I ran into him again, he looked at me, and I knew he remembered. This time I ran to the bathroom and began to sob.

I sent a text to my supervisor from work (as I had shared with her about seeing him the first time) and she sent me some comforting messages back. When I felt it was safe, I left. Sadly, I kept returning. Because I had been programmed to believe that I needed to be in church to be good enough for God, I kept exposing myself to this week after week. Looking back now, I am sad that I allowed it. I am sad I didn't know I could choose to not attend any more, that I could take care of myself. It was as if my trauma was convincing me that I was wrong for believing what happened, or wrong for interpreting it as rape, and that I should just allow this man to continue to cause me to feel bad about myself. Slowly, eventually, I stopped going. I began to wake up on Sunday mornings and realize I did not need to expose myself to this. It was freeing once I made the choice. I believe it was those moments of seeing this man, coming face to face with him at this moment in my life, that I realized I had to get help. Real help. I started therapy again, and sought help for my healing.

In this healing experience I have had to push myself to want to heal some of the trauma with my dad, even in his death. Even though it is somewhat hard to call it trauma, I know that I must call it what it is. It was early December 2021, and I was starting to feel my dad's presence strongly in my meditations. Then he started to show up and began talking to me. I know for some this might sound strange, that my father who has passed away, who is no longer living, is coming to me talking to me about trauma in my life, but I fully believe this has happened and my experiences have been real. In the process of growing in my awakening I came to understand that we really do have spirit guides, and they have always been with us. Once I learned that my guides wanted to communicate with me and help guide me in my life, I began to allow them to. Just like God, they are loving energy and never force themselves into the human experience.

The first time I heard from my dad was just a few short months after he passed. I was still not sure what I believed about the afterlife. I was out on a hike and really praying. I connect with nature easily and that day was no different. It was a windy day and many of the trees were blowing in the wind, their leaves rustling, a familiar, soothing sound for me. As I walked, I connected with a particular tree on the trail, feeling as if it wanted to communicate with me. This wasn't anything new for me, as I always loved trees. This day, I stopped, hugged the tree, felt my connection with it and named it. I would come back to it many more times after that to meditate and heal at times I felt alone or needed to grieve. After I had my moment with this tree, I continued to walk, looking around for things to take pictures of, and I noticed there were some beautiful big rocks along the side of the trail. But when I stopped by these rocks something strange happened. A tree, not far in the distance off the trail, began to make some sounds. It was bending and creaking almost as if it was trying to get my attention. I kept walking and ignored it at first but then something in me said to go back. So I turned around and went back to the larger rocks I had noticed and sat on them. Maybe this tree had something to tell me as well. As I sat there, I reached up and held onto my necklace with a pendant of the moon. It had been a gift from a friend with the phase of the moon on the night I was born. As I held it, I heard a voice, "I loved you since the day you were born." At first, I thought I made it up. I turned to look at the tree behind me that had been making the strange noises and realized maybe the tree had me come back to listen to something. Then I heard the voice again. "I've loved you since the day I saw you born." *Dad!?* Could it really be? I started to listen closer. The only thing I could think of was my dad was trying to talk to me. I always carry a bag with me when I hike and that day was no different. I happened to put a journal and pen in my bag before I left, which I pulled out and started to write down what I was hearing. I heard the same thing again and then I realized it was my dad. I heard him say to me, "I always loved you, Ang." At that I began to sob. My dad was talking to me. I questioned this several times afterwards, but it wasn't long after this that I would realize it really did happen. I still know what tree it was, and now I have made a memorial for my dad by collecting rocks for him and taking them to him each time there is a holiday. Since he was cremated, we do not have a special place to go and so I have made that our place.

It was probably five months after this that my dad's spirit came to see me again. This time in a vision just as I was waking for the day. In this vision, I saw myself running onto a basketball court, full of many people. But as I ran around the edge of the court it became empty, like no one else was there. I first ran into an old teacher from high school that I was close to and still am, and stopped to say hi and visit with her. After I visited with her for a moment, I started to rush to the other side as if I was late for a game and needed to get to the locker room and change. As I turned the corner of the court, I looked up to see my dad standing about halfway down the court. I was shocked and stopped in my tracks, looking at him. I stood there for a moment and in my disbelief said, "Dad? Is that you?" He answered "Yes," with a huge smile on his face. I said, "But you're dead!"

In this vision, my dad had on blue jeans and a blue and white pinstripe shirt, his hair was gray as it had been as long as I knew him, but was a bit younger than when he passed away, maybe in his fifties looking really handsome like he always did, and he seemed completely healthy. Since my dad had died of cancer, being able to see him like this was a relief. I ran to him and hugged him tightly, not wanting to let go. I was so excited to see him and so ready to just talk to him and be with him forever. He put his hands on my shoulders, pulled me gently away from him, looked at me in the eyes and said, "Ang, there is Nothing, No One, or Anything on this earth that you should be that upset about, or rushing that much for, because the only thing that matters when you get to this side is love. Let it go. It will be okay."

I was shocked. It was the best advice and clearest instruction I had ever gotten. He knew it was something I needed to hear. The next few moments I spent visiting with him about how his "heaven" experience was going, and after we visited for a while, I gave him a big hug and I began to walk away and leave him, walking towards the door I had originally been rushing to, but this time calmly. As I did, I remembered that he was "dead," and therefore I might not see him again, so I turned around quickly to look back and asked him, "But dad! You're dead! Can I really talk to you?" He smiled back at me and said, "As above, So below. You can manifest anything you want." I was so happy knowing I could talk to him anytime I wanted to that I ran back to give him another huge hug and thank him for coming to see me and for the advice he gave me, and to tell him, "See you later."

As I did this, I began to have this strange understanding that I was in a vision, and that my body was in my bed still. I noticed that my body was crying and grieving the fact that my dad was gone and dead, and I would not physically ever get to see him again. As I "hugged" my dad in the vision, I had so much peace, yet my body was in pain. My dad said to me, "I need to go, your body is getting upset." I looked up at him confused and then realized what he was saying. I was having an "out of body" experience, my spirit was in the vision while my body was still in bed asleep. I didn't want to leave him, but my spirit was much more peaceful and understood that it wasn't the last time I would be with him, only my body was weeping in sadness. It was such a strange feeling. As my spirit let go of my dad, I gave him one more goodbye and I love you, and walked off the court, turning as I did because I was curious to see where he would go from there. His spirit shot straight up into the air and vanished. He was back in what we call Heaven.

The next scene of my vision, I was walking out of the building and getting into a car with several people in my life I had felt betrayed by. The car was full of them, and I was in the backseat trying to be friendly and "hang out with them." But as I spent time with them and they interacted with one another, the things

I used to do to fit in or to feel a part of the group, I no longer had any interest in doing, and I just sat there as they engaged with each other. We drove off and the car pulled up to a long drive with two houses at the end of it. The drive was beautiful with trees lining it, and as a photographer I wanted to take pictures of the scene. I grabbed my phone as we all got out of the car to walk down the drive. But each time I went to take a picture, two of the women who had gotten out of the car with me, both friends I had once considered very close, kept getting in the way of my shots. I became irritated and struggled with getting the right photo. As one of them noticed me becoming irritated they turned and said in a mocking tone, "Oh, we are SO sorry, we didn't even know you were trying to take a picture. Here, let us move so you can get the perfect shot, because we know you are so good at pictures." Then they looked at each other and smiled as if it was an inside joke.

Normally, I would become even more irritated, but in this vision, I remembered what my dad said to me, and something clicked! I suddenly had a realization of the difference between real love and conditional, earthly love. This earthly love holds us back from being able to raise our vibration of love by clinging to stagnant energy around us, and most of us are unaware of this or are unwilling to raise our vibrations of love energy to another level. It wasn't that these were bad people or spirits around me, it was that they were not at the same place I was in my love journey any longer, and it was my (negative) attachment to them that was keeping me from my destiny and fulfilling my purpose in life. Once I had this realization, my anger and hurt turned to empathy and compassion. I went ahead and took that photo and continued down the path with them to the two houses.

At the end of the path, I had a choice. To go with them into the house on the right, which was beautiful and modern, but it would involve more interactions with these two individuals and others, or to walk a little further to the house on the left, off the drive a bit, situated in a wooded area, the path to it overgrown and rarely used. I, of course, decided to tell these ladies goodbye, and took the path less travelled. As I walked down that wooded path, the vision ended.

It was clear to me what my dad's message was to me that day. He actually came to give me several messages. One, that nothing on this earth was worth becoming overly upset about. That the stress, the anger, the bitterness, jealousy, judgment, hate, all that negative energy I was holding onto, rushing through life, hiding myself, was not worth it. That the only true thing that ever mattered was love, and now that he was on the other side, remembering who he really was, and experiencing his true spirit and purpose, he was coming to remind me—love is all that matters. Not the love we know here on earth, but a divine love. The most high energy of love you can imagine. I felt it when I hugged him. There is no explaining this love in a human language.

The other message he gave me was that we create our reality on this earth by what we think and what we seek. As above, so below. I can manifest anything I want on this earth. I can believe something and it can become my truth. Just as the teachings of Jesus tell us, seek and you shall find, that is what my dad was telling me. Speak it, and it is yours. Call on me, and I will come. Be present with me, and I will be present with you. Yes, Jesus, God, these are spirits, but so are our loved ones.

I have come to understand that just because religion taught me that this is negative or bad, it doesn't mean it is. That teaching is just something that was made up to keep us from knowing how to speak with spirits and understand things on a higher level outside of our ego minds. Religion wants to keep us bound under it so we follow it. Without followers, it is nothing. We do not need religious teachings to follow God. We need love. God is love. That is all. The other clear message my dad gave me was that my spirit is not my body. That my body can feel deep feelings of sadness and grief, and my spirit be completely at peace. These can happen simultaneously. Knowing what my body felt like in that moment when my spirit was hugging my dad, and how sad it felt, yet how peaceful my spirit felt, was something I will never forget. Our spirit is our true self, and that was what my dad wanted me to understand. The human emotions and ego, this body, these feelings, all of this fades away. That is why it is so important to live our lives at the highest vibrations of love energy we can while we are here in this body, because without that, we are not truly living as our authentic selves.

This leads me to one more vision I had with my dad. The one about judgment. The time he asked me for forgiveness. I had started to know how to connect with my dad's spirit more often through these experiences, and when I meditated on having him come through and spend time with me, it wasn't anything difficult. But then I started to find myself rejecting my dad's presence. I would sense him wanting to talk to me, but I would shut it down. Christmas was just around the corner and I started to wonder if maybe I was avoiding grieving something.

I had learned in my healing that avoiding feelings of grief was not good, so I decided that I would look inward to process my feelings and allow them to flow out of me. That day I meditated and began to allow myself to grieve. In the process of meditating I opened myself up to hearing from my dad as well, as I was feeling him wanting to talk to me. As I did, I heard in my spirit, "It is okay to heal and process our relationship and everything you experienced, you won't hurt me by processing this, and I cannot feel pain." As soon as I heard this, I knew it was my dad and I knew exactly what it meant. It was time to actually go back and remember what I had blocked out of my memories to protect myself. It was time to heal my wound from my father, and all those mental blocks I was not allowing myself to heal because they were painful for me to remember. I knew I needed to process how my dad made me feel and stop holding on to the negative feelings I created about myself due to that. It was time to heal that part of my history. I knew I needed to tell my therapist that part of my history and open up about all the times in my life I felt invisible because of his neglect. He had given me permission to do this, and I knew it was needed. I was somewhat nervous about telling her, as I still often worried about what people thought about my spiritual awakening and being able to hear from spirits. Would she believe me? Would she think I was crazy? Could I share this stuff with her? It was a battle to determine to share that part of my story with her, but I did share it. It ended up being a peaceful moment, and it felt freeing to open up about these things. She was open and loving in her response, believing me. I processed some that night with her but knew it would need to be processed some more another time to fully heal from it. Still, I had begun and that was what mattered.

Later that same week I had another experience with my dad regarding this same subject. I was processing forgiveness and thinking about my trauma. I felt as if my dad wanted to speak to me again, so I stopped what I was doing to meditate. As I got my mind quiet my dad came in without hesitation and began to speak very clearly to me about forgiveness and the power of it.

Being a former religious follower I had heard much about forgiveness in the church. Forgive one another and you shall be forgiven, confess your sins to be forgiven, and Jesus dying on the cross for us sinners was the ultimate story of forgiveness, without which no one is able to go to heaven. Then there are the other examples in the bible such as Mary Magdalene being told to go and sin no more after being ousted because she had been with many men, and the man on the cross beside Jesus making it into heaven just at the last moment before death because he cried out to Jesus. I always wondered what happened to that man on the other side. Did Jesus not care what happened to him? Outside of these teachings, we don't really see Jesus doing actual acts of forgiveness. There is some debate that some of these stories were added on by later church leaders to make Jesus appear to be different than he was to add more followers to their church and to give more control to the clergy. The one teaching on forgiveness that I do resonate with is when Peter asks about forgiveness. If the story is translated correctly, the writer tells us about how Peter asks Jesus about forgiving his brother, and how many times he shall do so, and Jesus answers back, "seventy times seven." If we were to translate seventy times seven in the language we use now, it means always, without limit.

There are so many ways to look at the topic of forgiveness that one could debate it from many different views and perspectives. Forgiveness toward other people, and forgiveness for sins. Then there is the Lord's prayer, "Forgive us our sins…" Some believe they must confess sins to someone dedicated in the church, while others believe they can go straight to God and ask for forgiveness. I've often wondered how many of those who feel required to confess their sins to other humans feel they ought to confess the sins on the list such as gossip or gluttony.

With all the different beliefs and interpretations of forgiveness, it can feel overwhelming and confusing to know which is right and which is wrong. Which religion is teaching the right way and which one is not? I know I spent many hours confessing all the things I did wrong. If you're anything like me, the idea of confessing sins and asking forgiveness for all of them could seem quite daunting. With so many layers of understanding of forgiveness developed over hundreds or thousands of years, I had only known what I had been programmed to know, and I am sure you are the same.

As I was having this experience with my dad, and he was speaking about forgiveness and the power of it, I began to think about all of this—all my prior knowledge about forgiveness and what counted as forgiveness and what didn't. Everything shifted for me at that moment. Everything I believed about forgiveness changed in an instant and through my dad's spirit I came to understand forgiveness on a level I had never known before. The way my dad spoke to me about forgiveness was as a divine expanded love energy that I had no idea could even exist. The actual power of forgiveness is so profoundly deep that the human ego and mind can have no true understanding of how powerful it is.

I suddenly had an awareness and understanding of the reason the man Jesus actually came to this earth—the real reason for his message, the gospel of love. Suddenly I got it on a different level than I ever had before. Forgiveness is so divinely powerful, it not only frees us here on earth, but it also frees the spirits of those who have passed on. I now understand forgiveness as a transition in the energy of love—moving from the form of a human body containing our spirit, to a more free emanation of energy, love, light, highest self, spirit. We truly never die. That day, my dad spoke to me about forgiveness and as he did my awareness expanded to see our true selves, our spirit selves, in what we might call heaven. And to move into a higher dimension and understand God's love, or the energy of love, you must experience forgiveness.

In this vision it was as if I stepped out of my body and into a Heavenly realm. Like I joined my dad. It was the most intensely powerful vision I had had so far. Because of what he was talking about and how it didn't just affect me, but also him, it hit me differently.

161

I sobbed and sobbed as he said spoke to me: "Your forgiveness will give me the power to move into the higher vibration of love I am seeking and the purpose of why I lived the life on earth as your father."

As I heard these words, I immediately thought of all the teachings on forgiving one another and the power of it. How it releases us from the very pain keeping us disconnected. I know there are teachings not just in Christianity about this, but other cultures as well. This was such a divine moment for me, and my spirit was so connected with my dad's that I physically could feel his longing for me to forgive him. Not that he was in pain, or that he needed to be released from anything painful, but that he longed for me to understand what it was like to be in a higher vibration of love myself, and for that there needed to be forgiveness.

Because there is no pain, no suffering, no sadness, or anything in the higher realms other than love energy, which we call Heaven, all the forgiveness has to happen on this earthly level. So I am the only one that can grant this to him.

He also explained that spirits come to earth to learn that level of love through forgiveness. Without the experience of forgiveness, we have no idea how to relate to God's love because in the higher realms we have no need for it. There, we are never outside of God's love and cannot know exactly what it is because for our spirits, it just IS. My dad explained that he needed to know what it was like to be loved and then forgiven by someone at a lower vibration to get to this understanding, and now that he was in the higher realms without any understanding of time or concepts of it, he could now look back at his entire lifetime and see all the things that happened from beginning to end. He was able to see what hurts he caused me and what pains I was still working through. He asked me to continue to work through the traumas he caused me and that as I work through them, through the process of forgiveness, it not only allows me as a human to find freedom, but he as a spirit to increase his frequency of love, becoming a higher being in the heavenly realms.

This lined up exactly with what I experienced in the previous vision I had with my dad a few months prior when he told me that nothing truly mattered outside of love, that holding onto anything else was going to cause me pain and suffering and that is not the plan for the spirit. As we grow and become more aware of our higher consciousness and connectedness with the energy of love, we begin to allow our spirits to lead us rather than our egos. It also allows us to heal our traumas, decreasing our triggers and changing how we show up in experiences that remind us of past hurts.

But if one does not fully get to this place in the human lifetime, then the spirit will likely seek to expand that awareness of higher consciousness through situations or connections that help open us up. Some do get stuck in between earth and heaven and it may take a while before this is released. That is why you may feel the presence of many lifetimes of generational traumas being passed on because it was truly never healed or dealt with. My dad is trying to help heal this pattern through me. I do not believe he is a stuck spirit, but a free one, coming to bring awareness to what can happen when I work through healing my trauma, forgiving him and others who have harmed me in my life, and continuing my journey in awakening my spirit by connecting with my higher consciousness.

Judgment

Most of us at some point have heard the concept of different levels of heaven. In the past, I did not give it any thought. Now I have come to understand there is some truth to the idea. When my dad explained to me that forgiveness would help him to rise to another level of energy, frequency, and love, I caught a glimpse of it. Because we exist within the matrix of societal limitations and the boundaries of earth and our forms on it, we can be stuck in a very limited understanding, unable to see anything outside the scope of our programming. We hear about things that might seem a little bit odd, or woo-woo, and dismiss it because it doesn't fit in our box that we've been taught to think inside of. Over time we may be able to expand our box a bit, and now and then change a few of our beliefs and understandings about things, accepting new things we didn't accept before, but all of this is still in the realm of our limited human understanding and egoistic thinking.

Even looking back at the list of sins, we tend to do this. I think of things such as thinking a tattoo is bad, damaging the body that God gave you and because your body is the temple of God you must never get one. Then in the progression of the box getting bigger, maybe switching to a different line, starting to believe it is okay to get a tattoo if it is honoring God. It is interesting that we can easily be trained in our thinking to believe something is good or bad all based on a belief. Even to believe that our body is a temple, that a body that decays, and returns to dust, gets scars, holds in trauma, might one day be resurrected and used again. Yet in our lifetime, we might avoid a tattoo while we fill our body with junk food every day, and don't take care of it in other ways. I remember at times having speakers come into the church and some of them being very unhealthy people, talking about healing and the love of God. I often wondered exactly what kind of healing they could manifest as they did not take much care of themselves. I am one of those people that believe you should practice what you preach. I have a hard time listening to someone who does not do so.

The box our mind has created is so small that we have no idea what is on the outside, or that we even are living inside one. There is literally no way to know what is possibly happening on the outside of our boxes because we are too focused on the four walls created on the inside of the box, making sure it looks polished. Most of us are ready to argue and protect our box when it gets pushed up against. Especially the corners of the box, the parts that are tender, maybe where trauma occurred in our lives and we have not fully acknowledged we need healing in that area and have just placed it on the altar for God to heal. Those tend to be the touchy subjects that trigger us and cause us to have a reaction. I have a feeling this book might be doing that for a few people.

It is not my intention to cause you pain, but to help educate and help you to see a different way of viewing the world around you, not just physically but spiritually. The divine energy of love is so much bigger than a box. And the fact that I have been blessed to even possibly be able to see some of the outside of the box I live inside, makes me want to help others see outside of theirs as well. I feel so honored to be given this privilege and I know it is my calling to now share it with you. So, I know this can be triggering to hear, but please know, this all comes from genuine love. Because I myself have been there. Coming from a place of compassion and much trauma in my life, I lived most of my life in a box, blinded by its walls, but at times doing it comfortably because I thought it was keeping me safe. Fear kept me in the box, believing that what was outside of it was evil. Since I had already experienced a lot of evil in my life and I didn't want to experience any more, I dared not look outside of my walls. Even if you haven't experienced a lot of trauma in your life, you may fear being outside of the programmed box. It doesn't even take religion to develop the programming box. It can come from anything in our lives. Schools, family traditions, cultural beliefs, the area you live in. So many things we experience in this life develop who we are as humans, and without an expanded view outside of those things, we have no clue what it is like to live outside of those walls.

As my dad began to speak to me about this forgiveness, I began to feel something deep inside of me that I could not explain in earthly words to you. It was as if I was floating and completely surrounded by a warm, comforting, mellow, vibrant, clear, shining white light. There is no other way to describe this. I have no other words than divine love energy. The love was so insanely intense that it cannot be compared to any love felt on this earth. I tried to find words to explain this once, and the only way I could come close was by taking every single positive emotion you could have and experiencing it all at the same time. I believe there are a few humans that have felt this love maybe through a near death experience or by remembering their pre-birth. I believe children might even know this love. This feeling of love was so insanely intense, it was so desired, that I almost wanted to just go into it, stay forever, and not worry about continuing my life on earth.

In my meditation my dad began to share with me and asked me to work toward forgiving him. In my exchange with him I told him that I had already forgiven him and that I thought that once you had forgiven someone it was done and over and that there really wasn't anything else to do. My dad then explained to me in more depth what forgiveness really is. That is when he began to explain to me what judgment was. It was nothing that I had previously been taught to believe.

This is what he shared with me. Forgiveness is letting go, not just that person, but all the hurts. You often hear that forgiveness is not for the other person but for you. This is true, forgiveness frees you. It gives you the opportunity to heal. But what I came to understand that day was that in order for true forgiveness to happen, you must then allow yourself to fully heal from the experience that caused you to need to forgive. This is what got me, this is where I completely broke down in tears and began to understand forgiveness in a more divine way. As my dad continued to have this exchange with me, he explained to me that forgiveness is not just for us humans. Forgiveness is for those who have passed on as well. Forgiveness is for humans on earth as we do the healing work, but it is also for spirits. Forgiveness frees those spirits who are in their judgment period, which actually allows them to move into the next understanding of love and into the higher dimensions of energy in becoming a higher spirit in the heavenly realms.

As I have said many times before, this can be confusing because we think in human terms when we think of this. I have come to understand that we cannot fully understand anything in the subtle or higher or heavenly realms of reality from a limited human perspective. We are unable to understand that there is no hierarchical system in heavenly realms like there is on this earth.

We humans have tried to create a simulacrum of heaven based on what we "think" heaven looks like, because deep inside of us our spirits remember something about layers, energy, and moving higher. The only thing our human brains can think of is to create a system that "looks" like what our spirits remember in heaven and the structure of it. But all we can remember is that there are layers, and there is a system, and there are some things that seem bigger or better than others, and there is a head and things under it. Our spirits know that our purpose is to become more like God in our love, but our human ego gets in the way of this. Because our ego self is not connected to or surrendered to our spiritual self, our ego begins to create its own interpretation without the spirit and therefore creates hierarchical systems of religion and politics, castes and classes, systems that generate things such as war, murder, racial injustice, white supremacy, rich and poor, man over woman, fat and thin, etc. It is the human ego that has developed hate. Our minds cannot wrap around this concept of a divine love, a divine energy, and true forgiveness without a system of give and take, so we created our own system on earth to try to recreate what we felt in our spirits.

This is really the reason Jesus came to the earth, to try to remind us of and to reconnect us with our true higher selves, our spirit. But the ego man rebelled against this, killing him, as humans desired to continue engaging in hierarchical systems of control and power. When we step outside of this programmed mind and ego self, connecting with our true spirit, this is where we find our true healing, our true understanding of divine love energy, and really know what forgiveness is about—the purpose of life on earth. What Jesus came to remind us of was who we really are. What Buddha tried to teach us was to connect to our higher self by quieting the mind. We all will go back to this place where the spirit lives. None will avoid it; no human body will overcome decay or death, which releases again to where the spirit is free. It is where our spirit came from and where it will return to. Therefore, it is not our body that is made in the image of God, but our spirit. Our body is not the temple of God that needs to be protected, it is just a temporary holding place that we must learn to overcome and train through our spirit, becoming our higher self through developing an understanding of how to connect with our higher consciousness, decreasing the ego, and then being led by the spirit through the energy of love.

As I mentioned before, I have come to learn that true forgiveness and healing doesn't just heal us individually and from past trauma, but allows those who have passed on to move through their own judgment period, in which they personally are judging their own lives. It is not God that is standing beside them judging them, but themselves. Since this experience I've also had connections with other loved ones who passed—in my meditations others visited me.

My mother sadly did not grow up with her father, but when she was in her early thirties she found out he was in Texas. I remember being very young at this time and traveling from Kansas to Texas to meet him for the first time. I remember stopping in Oklahoma to meet a sister she learned about, and then spending time in Texas meeting her brother and her father as well as other relatives. We have stayed in touch with some of these family members over the years, but it was not until then that we knew about them. My mom, not having her dad growing up, had known her stepdad as her dad, and I knew him as my grandpa. I never knew my biological grandpa as my own grandparent.

During one meditation, as I was quieting my mind, several spirits showed up at once. I was not seeking out any spirit to come and visit me, so it was a surprise. There were four of them and a dog. I knew the dog right away. It was my dog, Bud, that we had when I lived with my stepdad. I had heard that animals could come through and talk to you in the spirit but I wasn't sure. Bud came to me, bringing to my awareness something I had experienced with him. He was coming to help me in my healing process. I had forgotten about the experience and my dog had come to let me know that it was okay, that I struggled in those years of being in that house, and that I often found comfort in spending time with him. His visit also helped me feel at ease about other things I've struggled with in my life, worried that I was a bad person, but now understanding that those behaviors arose out of my trauma and abuse. I was thankful for the short exchange with Bud, and he walked away.

Then the spirit of a man walked towards me out of those present. I did not recognize this spirit or have any particular feelings of connection with it. It was just the presence of a male person. Then as it began to speak to me I realized who it was. It was my mom's dad. My biological grandpa. He said to me that he was sorry. He apologized for not being there for me. I was confused when he said this and almost angry at him, and said back to him that it wasn't me he wasn't there for, but my mom, and because of that he caused much trauma in my mom's life. He confirmed this and shared more detail with me. He then explained to me that because he had left my mom, he had also left me, and that he was supposed to play the role of my grandparent in my life on earth during that lifetime, but he had not fulfilled his role. He also did not fulfill his role of being a father to his daughter, my mom, and he was sorry for the hurt he caused, and asked me for forgiveness. I didn't feel sad for myself, but I did for my mom, realizing that she had missed out on having a dad just as I did. My grandfather then explained to me the generational trauma developed over time in the blood line I was born in, and that there needed to be a healing of the father's wound. That by me forgiving him, and my forgiveness of my own dad, I was also helping to heal many generations of fathers leaving their daughters and their sons in their lives. I then realized that my dad also experienced this with his dad. I am not fully sure how many generations this went back, but I do know that there is much trauma on both sides of the family and it is now something I desire to learn more about. In my understanding of forgiveness, and getting myself outside of the box religion taught me about it, I now understand that in my forgiveness I am not just healing my wounds, but the many generational wounds passed on in our family bloodline. For some reason, I picked this family to be born into, fully knowing I would experience this and I would be the one to heal it. I, of course, would not know this until these moments and in my awakened state. Now through my own healing, and working through trauma, I am coming to understand how to manifest healing not just for myself, but for many others that have gone before me, and those still on the earth needing to work through their healing process.

By doing the healing work within myself, I am allowing those who have passed on and transitioned back to heaven to continue their work on understanding the divine love of God, and if there is such a thing as reincarnation, to know that if they choose to come back to this earth, they can experience something different this time. They do not have to go through the abandonment of a parent. This is what Jesus meant as well, "by my stripes you are healed." I am not saying I am comparing myself to Jesus at all. I do believe Jesus to be a highly developed spirit and energy of love that is much higher than most. I also believe this to be so about many other spirits that have come and gone. But I know that in my healing, in my wounds, in my stripes and healing, in opening up my wounds and allowing them to bleed once again to get out the infections, I am allowing healing to happen in my spirit, and doing it not just for those who have transitioned over to move into a higher level of expanding their love energy and divinity, but for the hope of helping many others heal as well on the earth. As very hard as this process is, I am happy to be a part of it.

You see, forgiveness is so much more powerful than what we give it credit for. Judgment is nothing that we humans make it out to be. It is not this evil moment in heaven where God decides if we get to stay or go. It is our own spirit's process of remembering and growing in the frequencies and energies of love. We humans, in our ego minds, throw the words around so carelessly. But in reality, forgiveness and then judgment both have such a divine higher power of energy and love. When we truly walk in this love energy, allowing it to flow through us in an authentic way, we heal not just ourselves, but each other on earth too. We can diminish hate, self-absorption, jealousy, controlling one another, racism, taking another human and using them for our own pleasure, and religion would cease to need to exist. We would likely really start to understand what Jesus came to talk about, what he meant when he said, I am that I am.

This is something I also came to understand in my meditations. We choose to experience this human life to experience God's love. My dad, in his pureness wants to understand God's love so fully, he exposed himself to pain. In his humanness, his ego, just like everyone's ego does, became full of trauma and programming, so he was unable to fully give me the love I needed as a daughter. He saw this when he got to the other side. He also did not know I had been abused or experienced all the other things I had in my life. Once he fully saw the experiences in my life, and all I had gone through in his absence, he allowed himself to go through that process of pruning and judging to become his highest spirit self and grow. This again is not something our human minds can fully understand, but I came to understand that our religious beliefs and thinking, developed over time, that stated that God judges us and sends wrath on us for all of our wrongs, is not true. God is love. God is unable to be anything other than Love. We humans are the ones that experience all the other lower vibrations of painful energies and judgments. God allows us to go through the pruning experience because this energy of God loves us so much it wants to bring us into the full understanding of what that energy actually is, what the truth of divine love energy is. Slowly, over the many experiences we have on earth, we go through that refining process and expand our understanding, developing our higher self and growing in spirit. Without the human experience, there is no other way to fully know true love.

The Frequency of Love

As I study and learn more about our soul journey on this earth, I come to understand the ancient ways of life: watching and following the stars and the alignment of the planets, noticing when they appear to stop and start again; the moon's phases, the sun's cycle, the sky's clouds and the patterns of life; how the waves of the ocean and plants provide healing and oxygen; what nourishes the body and what causes it harm; how to embrace another human in authentic love, and how to set a healthy boundary to keep yourself in authentic love; how to live in true harmony with everything around you, staying connected with your higher self; how to live off the land and share resources with others without a scarcity mindset, knowing that when we honor nature it continues to supply our needs; how nature continues to provide all the resources needed for itself and humanity when it is respected and taken care of; that nature actually provides the medication needed to heal the body by grounding, being present in it, and using its resources. The threat of climate change would cease to exist if we were to give reverence to the created energies in nature as we do to religious teachings.

In ancient times people worshiped Mother Earth and Father Sky, trusting they would work together to provide the rain and connect in perfect harmony, vibrating in the love frequencies that were creating the very moment of existence. There was a respect for plants, understanding the unity of growth and decay, that compost provides nourishment to the plants that remain growing. There was an understanding of the cosmos, the skies, the orbits of the planets, and people knew how to read the stars to see the seasons and predict events on the earth. There was an embrace between humans and animals, an understanding that it was for the good of nourishing the human body if they must kill and eat one, giving respect to the animal and only killing if it was to be used for good, only needed if there was a lack of resources in other areas. It seems we have gone away from the mindset of reverence to a mindset of greed. We even forget to respect one another and the value each person has. Most of us don't even live by our core values, though we hold others to them and judge them with scorn.

We must revere the earth in all its glory, vibrating in the highest love energy and frequencies, working in complete harmony, in order to recognize that we, too, can live the same way. I envision these times, almost as if I have experienced them, and maybe I did, many lifetimes ago. I know there is a calling from Mother Earth, asking us to come back to the truths of love; for us to turn our eyes from darkness to the light vibrations reflecting off the land and trees; to hear the whispers of the forest, and the breeze singing the praises of the heavens above, a universal love calling all to become one; to embrace the human soul above the human flesh, seeing past skin color or the illusion of race. While I was in the church, I heard teachings that suggested a time of peace and unity on earth would be suddenly interrupted by God's judgment and wrathful destruction, raising up only "true believers" and leaving the rest behind to suffer. But I think those are ideas of men who wished to create fear among their people so as to maintain authority and control.

I now understand that our souls have come to
earth to experience human life in order to be exposed
to a low energy vibration, and through it to awaken
an understanding of God's abundant love. Without
such a lowly dark place, away from God, away from
the love vibrations of heaven, our souls cannot
experience such a deep pit of despair. It is only on
earth that we find a place where we forget who we
are. Without the true connection to the highest of love
energy, and the deepest connection to the truest
source of love that connects all things, we, being at
the lowest vibration, are forced to go deep within
ourselves to seek what true love really is—to find the
spark and bring it to life. Our spirit that lives deep
inside never forgets—it is what keeps us seeking,
and through our seeking we are able to find. It is true:
those who seek, find.

Here on earth we have given that spark the
name of spirit, or soul. However, lost in this human
existence over millions of years, that spark has
become hidden beneath egoic mind. Attempting with
our limited minds to regain awareness of our inner
spark and figure out how God would do things, we
began to create stories to explain our sense of
separation, and hierarchies in imitation of our ideas
of heaven and God. We made God a Man. We forgot
and misrepresented the Higher Realm beings we

once were before coming to the earth, creating a hierarchical system to live up to, consisting of senseless rules and structures, and a God of destruction and hate that would condemn humans to a place called hell. Our souls still knew who we were but the ego had taken over. We created places of worship, buildings, thrones, idols, leaders, and those who could intervene with God for us, as we slowly transformed God into a deity who would only love a human if they followed the rules and regulations created by human hierarchy. Slowly, we took the power away from our own spirits and gave it to the ego, forgetting the love that we had left heaven to come here and learn about. Everything became about control instead of love, about being obedient, about hierarchy, and slowly over time the spirit of love was suffocated by the ego.

I believe that is where Buddha and Jesus stepped in. And there have been many other such teachers over the millennia. Buddha had a very clear understanding of that vibrational love that we are all seeking. Many in Western culture have no true understanding of what the Buddha taught, or the teachings behind what we call Buddhism. Many believe that Buddhism is a "religion" and that a Buddhist worships Buddha. But really, Buddha was a teacher, and the founder of Buddhism, which is a practice, not a religion at all. Many of his teachings are very much like Jesus' and both men taught some of the very same concepts. Some of my favorite teachings and quotes are from Buddha, such as:

Every morning we are born again, what we do today is what matters most.

I had the privilege of spending time in Southeast Asia as a young adult. The first time I went to India—I was only seventeen. This was shortly after my "acceptance of Jesus" and I am surprised the church I was attending let me go. However, it was a highlight of my life and would forever change my view of the world. It set my foot on a path that I believe is still impacting me. A few years later, I traveled to Laos for several months and then a couple years later, to Thailand. My time in Southeast Asia was something that opened my eyes to Buddhist culture. I remember my first experience in India observing this completely different culture. India seemed rushed in some areas, very poverty stricken in others, with some areas that seemed very wealthy. It was the first time I saw what real poverty looked like—walking through the slums of India, the smells, the people, the looks on their faces, how they wanted to touch my skin because it was a different color. All these things imprinted themselves on my young mind. Sometimes I long to go back as an adult to experience this again, to see how I might show up differently. I believe the way I showed up then was more in shock than love.

Laos and Thailand are similar, but the people seemed to be much less rushed and stressed. My time in Laos impacted me the most. People were calm and spacious, coming and going as they pleased. No one seemed especially troubled by my desire to keep something on task. I would make an appointment for 3 p.m. and they would show up whenever they felt like it, usually many hours later, with no apology. It didn't seem to faze them at all. They appeared to enjoy the moment, just being present in the here and now. This mindset was a little contagious. I noticed that I stopped worrying so much about when things would happen during the day. I would just allow it to happen as it did. My stress decreased, my life settled, and I began to enjoy the days as they came.

I was there during the monsoon season, so it was raining almost the entire month I was there. I carried an umbrella with me everywhere. I had no vehicle, only walked places. At first, I was annoyed by the rain, but as I began to embrace the culture more, I started to enjoy it. I began to take in the smells of the nature around me. I started to look around at the abundant green and how the rain was bringing life to things. I embraced the moments when the rain stopped and enjoyed how the rain would cool the air when it came again. Learning to be present in the moment was something I wanted to take back with me to America. It was then I began to pay more attention to the temples around me as well. There were statues of Buddha everywhere. I could walk around the small town in just a few hours, so I could see all the temples in the city within a day. They were very quiet places. People that went to them took their shoes off before entering and would burn incense and get on their knees or sit cross legged and appear to be praying. I didn't know anything about meditation at the time.

The Buddha statues I saw there did not look like the ones we had in America. There were other figures as well that I did not recognize. I still don't know who they represented, but in my awakening and decreasing fear of the myriad goddesses and gods people around the world call upon, I have come to understand that there are different higher powers people look to as a source of security and help. I still don't know much about these teachings and philosophies but I do know that there is a clear difference between Hinduism and Buddhism, which at one point I did not. In India, they practiced mostly

Hinduism, while in Thailand and Laos it was Buddhism. Similar in some ways, but also very different. Much like the Christian faith in Europe and the Americas. I think we forget how many different sects of Christianity there are. We so easily judge other cultures for their multiplicity of faiths while looking past our own differences. The western culture is quick to judge. I wasn't sure I found a lot of judgment in the other cultures when I was there. Or at least they did not seem to judge me. Maybe I did not spend enough time there. I do know that at times they feared my religion. I am sad about that.

Hinduism and Buddhism are two religions with many similarities and many different concepts. They both involve the fundamental idea of oneness, as well as the idea of reincarnation, souls migrating through different lives and evolving along the way. They also both contain the idea of karma, or cause and effect, which relates to the idea of oneness because everything we do and even what we don't do has an effects on others, on the whole. Both were developed in India, although Buddhism migrated to other countries such as China, Japan, Tibet, and many other smaller countries in the region. In every place Buddhism spread, the different cultures influenced how the religion showed up in those places. Consider how different Tibetan Buddhism is from Zen Buddhism in Japan. On the outside they look totally different. Hinduism in India was influenced by a very hierarchical culture that involved a rigid caste system as well as a demeaning view of women. In spite of all these differences, and the various cultural influences on the teachings, there is truth within them as well, just as there is in the Christian religion.

We find many differences between the Christian faiths around the world, from Roman Catholicism to Eastern Orthodox, to Protestantism of many kinds, to Quakerism, Mormonism, and non-denominational churches. Each believes they have the "true" interpretation of who and what God is, and the true teachings of Jesus. Similarly, there are differences in Hinduism and Buddhism, but many of their fundamental principles are the same.

I find myself resonating with Buddhism because the practices of mindfulness, meditation, and the eightfold path, have been very beneficial for my healing of trauma and grief.

The eightfold path is the following: 1. Right view, 2. Right intention, 3. Right speech, 4. Right action, 5. Right livelihood, 6. Right effort, 7. Right mindfulness, 8. Right concentration.

The path begins with the right view, also called right understanding. We need to see clearly where we are headed before we begin. Right intention means the resolve to follow this path. Right speech and right action refer to what we say and do—to not harm other people or ourselves with our words and behavior. Right livelihood means how we live day to day, making sure our habits and our work don't cause harm to ourselves or others. Right effort refers to focusing our energy on the task at hand. Right mindfulness means awareness of the mind and body with discernment. With mindfulness, we might pause and consider whether what we are doing is harmful to ourselves or others. Finally, right concentration refers to dedicated practice, whether it is meditation or chanting. In other words, once we have directed our minds and lives toward awakening, we can proceed. Though the eightfold path is always listed in this order, it is not strictly sequential, and does not need to be followed in only this order.[1]

The eightfold path is a part of the journey I have taken towards healing my mind, body, and spirit, as well as learning to connect with my true self. It has also taught me many things about how my

[1] https://tricycle.org/beginners/buddhism/eightfold-path/)

consciousness works and the true meaning of life. Not only have these practices helped me connect with my consciousness, but they led me to understand the energy we hold in our bodies, which then led me to understanding the energy of our spirit. This energy has the ability to heal our body, mind, and spirit, and that same energy can help us heal from our traumas. Becoming familiar with this energy, I was able to discover Reiki which is a discipline within the Buddhist way of living and philosophy as well. I am thankful for the privilege of spending some time in Southeast Asia in my younger years and being exposed to some of these concepts in person.

I have many positive things to say about the teachings of Christianity and Jesus, but I also know how hard it is to see anything objectively through a fundamentalist lens. Breaking out of that mindset can be hard. One of the teachings in Christianity is that you must be involved in the church to be fully used by God, to keep yourself free from sin, and to prevent you from "wandering" away from God. Some churches push for people to be involved so deeply that they neglect their life outside of it. This approach can have a positive or negative impact, but in my experience, it often has a negative impact. Any human that is forced to neglect their true, authentic self and desires to follow the desires of another human is not living their highest calling. Sadly, I think parents, in the name of wanting the best for their children, take away their individuality instead, hindering their inner growth by programming them to do or believe only certain things. I do understand the desire to keep children close, and even the fear of them "wandering" away. What often happens, however, is that kids who are forced to attend church throughout their younger years feel restricted and suppressed by their teens, often rebelling (natural at that age) and no longer wanting to be a part of it. While it is natural for young adults to explore and wander for while to find their own place in the world, many of these kids feel they are going against their families at a much deeper level, challenging their whole paradigm, and the families can even shut them out because of their choices. This can create terrible rifts. It entangles love in a system of rules and regulations, which goes against what Jesus taught.

Our spirit is about connecting to God, not disconnecting. In spite of the high ideals of the churches, many young people find themselves pregnant before marriage or live in shame after marriage because they feel unable to live up to the rigid standards the church holds them to. This can cause cycles of shame, passed on to their own children, or they leave the church, never to return.

Some become more fundamentalist, more fearful and more shaming of others in their attempts to follow God or love God as they are called to do. The shame and blame cycle does not engender love and acceptance, nor faith that human beings can make mistakes and adjust and learn from them. It simply hinders authentic exploration, preventing young people from figuring out who they truly are, what their callings are in life, and then the cycle starts again.

Occasionally, there might be one in the family that breaks free from the religious cycle, and this one is often looked at as the outcast or the one that had not truly been a follower. Judgment and shaming seem to be easy when you do not understand someone's heart or reasons for doing what they are doing. I am always amazed at these stories. Some of the most amazing people I know have walked away from religion and live in their highest power of love. Before I had my awakening, I judged these people as wandering sheep who had lost their way. Now I am inspired by them. I recognize that they have somehow heard the calling of love and followed the prompting of their own spirit, connecting to a larger consciousness in a way that is rare and precious.

Finding this part of yourself is a tremendously profound experience. There often are no words to explain these moments. It can be difficult to share such an experience with others openly without sounding completely crazy or "woo-woo." It can feel like you've suddenly found this code to break out of the matrix and everyone else is still in it or in "that line" we talked about. It is tempting to grab them out of the line and show them how liberating it can be. But that's not how it works. You can offer perspective and even guidance to those who desire it, speak your own truth, but the experience of a true spiritual awakening is only known to the individual soul. No one can do it for another. Just as no one can truly heal another from their traumas.

As an awakening spirit, I do desire to provide comfort, to help in any way I can when someone is walking through the strange awakening stages, assuring them they are not alone, and are not crazy. I am so very thankful for the connections I found along the way that helped me. There were several moments in my awakening experience that truly had me questioning my sanity. Going from a religious mindset of believing I needed to be perfect all the time according to some rigid, arbitrary rules, to being free and true to myself no matter what, was the most liberating, exciting, excruciating, hard, healing experience I have ever had. I hear it gets easier the longer you are in it. I myself desire to never forget this part of the journey.

If you find yourself on this path, know that you are not alone, even though it may seem lonely. Know that you are not crazy even if it feels crazy. I ask the spirit to send you support and guidance and hope you can trust your intuition when you begin to sense you should go in one direction or another. I don't know how my spirit found the precious individuals who have helped me along the way—after my awakening happened, I was just drawn to certain people. Something in me led me to them, and I listened. They weren't always people physically near me. Many I found online. Others were close friends who happened to begin their own journeys around the same time I did or shortly after, and I just happened to mention something to them in passing that didn't scare them off, but helped them come out about their experiences too. I suddenly found myself teaching others about how to connect to their higher self, and things began fall into place. I was led to people that I could connect with on a soul-purpose level, and who could help me develop my own business. There would even be times I would have someone pop into my head who I had not talked to in years, and I felt compelled to reach out to them. I started to trust my intuition more and more, going with what I felt in my spirit, and about nine out of ten times I was led in the right direction. Noticeably, when fear and doubt crept in and I questioned my own clarity, that was most often when I was off.

Over time, as I continued to connect with my own spirit and learn about my consciousness and how to connect with my higher self, I began to learn about spirit guides. I also started to be drawn to tarot and oracle cards, crystals, and the use of a pendulum. When I realized that I had spirit guides I started to study how to connect with them and how to hear from them. Over time, I started to sense when they would tell me things or I would get ideas in my head that I felt they were leading me to do. I felt as if my spirit guides were encouraging me in my healing, and they would guide me in decisions I needed to make for my life. Never once have I been led the wrong way when I have taken the time to become quiet and seek direction from my guides, God, and my higher consciousness.

Trusting my higher self, trusting my guides, trusting my intuition has been challenging to move into as I have had to work intentionally and diligently to decrease my religious striving and really trust my spirit. I have found that in quiet moments, connecting with nature and trees, in meditation, practicing

mindfulness, in coming away from religion, I have
connected with the spirit more and been able to
understand love in a more profound way than I ever
would have in the church. Many of the teachings I
found within the four walls of the church not only kept
me from growing in my gifts but kept me from
believing I even had them, from speaking freely and
exploring the abilities I had. From energy healing to
intuitive abilities to reading energies in other people,
and predicting things before they may happen, there
are many experiences I have had that I cannot
explain away. The only way I can make sense of
them is to call them divine interactions or visions from
the divine source we call God.

During one of my meditations I had a vision my
spirit guides gave me of what it is like to step out of
our body and into a heavenly realm. During my
meditation I was doing some deep healing around
traumas I had processed in a recent therapy session.
As I sat there, I felt my guides gathered around me,
taking pain out of my physical body. It was a tense
moment, yet powerful and full of love. As I was in the
meditative state, I saw for the first time that one of my
guides was a feminine energy. She appeared as if
she was "in charge" of the other guides. She came to
me and began to place her hands on my stomach to
heal this area. I knew I could not have children. She

spoke to me and confirmed this, but gently filled my body with warming love and reminded me that it was not those who birthed physical children that had many children, but the barren women. I began to sob. This is a teaching you can find in the bible. It was a very healing moment for me and it came at a time I needed it.

I also began to understand more about my life purpose and calling through this. As I sat and allowed the healing process to happen, I was subtly ranking the guides according to who I thought had the most authority over the others. As the process of healing ended, the guides stepped back, a bit confused by these thoughts I was having. They explained to me that there is no hierarchical authority as we think of it in the human realm. Rather than one being above the other, they are all connected as one. They may have different qualities or roles, one may have a higher vibration, another might be brighter, or appear to have authority at a given time, but it has nothing to do with a ranking system. There is no need for that there, as there is only one ultimate source of energy, power, and love, and that is the Godhead. Outside of this source there is no control system, only a natural order in which all work together for the purpose of one another and the whole. The source of love is what keeps all energies, all spirits, all beings complete and connected—it does not matter how high or low the vibration of love is, it is all connected to the same source—none higher, none lower, all serving with the same love.

I had to shake off these ideas about a hierarchical system of any kind, such as a religious system or a political system, as the only means to keep order. Such systems are inherently flawed, leading to some being above others, imbalances in power, the search for control, the use of force. All of this works against the spirit, increasing pride and inflating the ego mind. Once I heard this from my guides, I had another very powerful vision, in which I could physically feel the power of the love energy.

I saw myself in a room that was completely white. It appeared to have nothing in it but a wooden chair. I sensed the chair slightly behind me to my right, but I wasn't able to see it very well because of how bright the room was, full of bright white light all around me. Suddenly windows appeared on all sides of the room, several on each wall, and through the windows came an even brighter light from the outside. I wondered how many more layers of bright there could be that exist. I could hardly see anything it was so bright. I noticed a door opening to my left with more light. I felt as if this light was wanting me to walk towards it, so I did. Once I started walking, I felt the urge to take the chair, so I grabbed the chair and dragged it to the door with me. As I got to the door, I began to step outside of my physical body, almost like unzipping my shell, shedding my body, and revealing only my spirit. As I took my physical body off, I sat it down on the chair, lifeless as if it was just a clothing item lying there, and turned back to the door.

I took a step out into this brighter light, realizing as I did so that my physical body was not capable of stepping into such a high frequency of love and energy. That was why I needed to shed my body to go into it. It was the highest form of energy and love I had ever experienced and I wanted to go into it deeper. There was nothing I wanted more. I tried to step forward to see what was around in the light and explore, but something prevented me and told me that I was only to experience the feeling, not come any further. I stopped and began to process my experience.

I was feeling into the meaning of human life and the processes of living and dying. It is the spirit's desire to experience this love, and in order to do so, it must plunge itself into the lower energies and vibrations first. Then its journey will take it through the lessons it needs to penetrate the blocks to each higher level of energy, vibration, and love. I had just experienced two of these higher levels in my meditation. Each higher form of vibration takes us to a higher understanding of God's energy of love. It is our ultimate goal to become spiritual beings of divine love, to love like God, and to conduct the highest of energies of this love. Our physical bodies are not usually capable of handling this and that is why they cease to go with us as we evolve. That is why they die.

I wondered why it is so difficult and rare for human beings to come to this understanding; why so much trauma comes into our lives, why we get stuck in our negative cycles and mindsets, why so many of us die with hate in our hearts, unforgiven and unforgiving, while others, a rare few, begin to awaken, to question, to take another path. I asked my guides what keeps some stuck while others are able to move out of it? They explained to me that there is a process of being able to achieve the highest goal, but in the process of trying to achieve that goal, many souls stop for a time. Some, for many lifetimes. But each soul has the free will to come and go as they please. Many choose to stay on the path of transformation. But many choose to stop and experience love in all forms of vibrations along the way. But no matter what, all beings, all things, are connected in this vibration of love. This opened me up to the possibility of reincarnation.

Had I not had these experiences for myself, I would think they were stories being told by a crazy person. But I myself, sane, stable in the process of healing, coming out of a religious mindset, had these experiences and know them to be true. I cannot tell you why, or how. All I can tell you is somewhere along my awakening experience I began to have access to spirit guides, angels, and those who have passed before me. In my previous thinking, I would have thought such a person was either possessed or crazy. But I speak and share from my own experience of the divine energy of love speaking directly to me. Nothing I experienced was scary or left me in fear. In fact, it gave me more peace, and that is what I hope it also gives you.

Free to be You

It wouldn't be fair to end this book without giving you some tools and a little advice about how to use the information I've offered through my story. I believe in practicing what I preach. I love to learn. I found throughout the process of writing this book that I felt the urge to research and learn more about what I was sharing so I could provide you with more evidence and information. My desire is to offer you good advice and effective education to help you in your healing. So when I saw a book that looked related to what I was writing about, or when someone suggested one, I would purchase it. Then, as soon as I started reading it, something wouldn't feel right, my body would tense up, and I would have to put the book down. The books were good and I liked them— it wasn't about that. But in my spiritual process I have learned to listen to my intuition and trust when my body gives me cues. The cue my body was giving me was to listen to and trust my own experience, not to seek advice or confirmation from others, but to believe I am worthy and to honor and respect what I know from going through my own healing. My body was telling me to keep it simple and keep it real.

I also came to understand how important a story is. The silence of my story was not just keeping me in bondage, but keeping others from their healing. I finally stopped seeking out the "professionals" and searching for others to guide me and began to understand that within myself I possess power and wisdom to share. In the process of writing this book, sharing my experiences, being honest, breaking my silence, I can provide healing not just for myself, but for any of you that feel led to read this. You will find a few things in this book that came from other resources, and from things I learned over the years as I worked in the field of mental health. I am thankful for the many years I spent working in the mental health field and the things I have had the privilege to learn under invaluable mentors. I also am thankful for the clients, who I learned the most from. However, nothing beats personal relationships; love is always the highest form of healing, and without it, healing is just bandage.

I noticed an amazing thing in the process of writing this book. I have always dreamed of doing some kind of work that would include helping people heal mentally, emotionally, and spiritually. When I was still operating from the perspective of the Christian church, I always dreamed this would include bringing people together and providing both the teachings of the bible and information regarding mental health together. As I have moved away from religion, I still reference the bible in many of the teachings I bring to my clients, and I very much love Jesus and the philosophies of life he brought to us. I believe that healing doesn't just require one layer of treatment. It requires many. You can't focus on just the human mind and body, or just the spirit in your healing.

Getting in touch with your higher self, your spirit, including love in your healing process, is vital. At the same time, receiving help from someone who understands trauma in the body is equally important, as well as the help of therapists who have done their own work and can stand in their own power of love during your healing process. Without all of it working together, it is like taking our scars, scraping off the top tissue, and not really digging into them and getting out the infections. The triggers and the cues remain in our body, continuing to infiltrate our lives in different ways such as sickness, anger, bitterness, and ongoing in cycles of self-sabotage.

At certain times in my healing journey I found myself feeling very exposed and vulnerable. It was as if the armor I had been wearing all my life had been taken off, and now I was standing on the battle ground fully exposed. Anyone could have access to me and stab me again because I was back in a child-like state where I was unarmored, yet as an adult. I had to retrain my brain and body how to feel safe without having to protect myself all the time, even in safe relationships. I had to learn how to set boundaries for myself and take care of myself without being defensive or closing my heart. Having some form of armor is good. The challenge is to create new, healthy habits to replace the old ones that are no longer useful.

Within the healing process, the body starts to dislodge energy stuck in destructive ways of thinking and acting, and this leaves the body in this open, exposed state. If we don't fill it with new, positive ways of thinking and acting, we may leave ourselves exposed to unhelpful influences. I believe this is a great example of what Jesus may have been trying to teach us when he talked about emptying ourselves of an evil spirit.

When an evil spirit leaves a person, it goes into the desert, seeking rest but finding none. Then it says, 'I will return to the person I came from.' So it returns and finds its former home empty, swept, and in order. Then the spirit finds seven other spirits more evil than itself, and they all enter the person and live there. And so that person is worse off than before.

As you can see, when the person rid themselves of the evil, they did not fill themselves back up with something positive and the evil returned and brought back even more evil. In my own understanding of these teachings, the evil spirits or demons are a symbolic way to describe negative energies, negative thinking, past traumas, or unhealed experiences in our bodies. Our bodies can manifest sickness because of trauma, not just physical traumas, but emotional traumas. Our bodies hold emotions inside of them and then they manifest physically. So when we do not deal with them, they become bigger.

So how do we fill our bodies back up with positive energies? By engaging in positive activities and mindfulness. Building ourselves back up, finding people that are positive for us, who lift us up rather than drain us. Engaging in activities that fill up our emotions with love and not despair. Learn healthy boundaries, and begin to love ourselves. Love is the biggest of all of these. Without truly loving yourself first, it really is not possible to do any of this. Once you love yourself, you can allow others to love you too. I remember this process being so hard to do for myself. It was why meditation was key in my journey—learning to be with myself without distraction. Learning to like myself was the challenge I needed to overcome. Once I began to love myself more, I was able to ask for help and to know what kind of help I needed. There was a time I would never ask for help, never let anyone know I was struggling or had a need. After I started to love myself, I wasn't as afraid to reach out and ask someone for support. For myself, because of needing to set many boundaries in my life, my therapist became that safe person. If you do not have a safe person, I highly recommend you find a therapist that can help you in this process. If you don't feel you can find one, then seek out a mentor. Do what it takes to find someone to help you. Even if it is on social media. This is how I began to seek friends to support me. There is no shame in looking for what you need. None of this is possible alone, and that was a hard lesson I had to learn myself. Don't leave yourself empty like Jesus said. Don't let yourself be filled back up with negative energies.

As you read in prior chapters you noticed several strange experiences I had in my awakening. I want you to know that you may not have the same experiences as I did. We all have different giftings and we all will have our own experiences. I don't want you to compare yours to mine. I do want you to find safe people to talk to about your experiences though. For myself, at first these scared me, and I was thankful for the few people I had to share them with. I wasn't sure what to think about them. Over time, as I learned to embrace these giftings and understand them, work with them, and use them for my highest good, I became more aware of my intuition and how to sense things more easily, which gave me an ease when I would have the experiences. In a way, it felt as if I was returning to my inner child, and all programming I had developed over my lifetime was being peeled off. It is possible this could happen to you on your healing journey. It is empowering in a way, but it is also not easy. I remember having a lot of strange things happening in my body. There would be days I wouldn't be able to eat much food, or days I felt ungrounded and knew I needed extra self-care and grace, or to be in nature to ground myself. Then there would be some days I knew I just needed to be in my own space to allow my mind to be quiet and process. I also found that sometimes there would be periods of healing that came when I would feel somewhat physically ill. I learned from other people in the process of healing that they, too, would report physical illness at times of deep healing or growth.

It may not happen for you this way, and your healing may not have moments like this. I only give you my experiences so you do not feel alone in yours. I was thankful to know I wasn't the only one. If you do not have someone to talk to about your experiences, there are some amazing communities on social media, and of course, I am always available too.

I have come to find in my own healing the importance of quieting the mind. My biggest encouragement for you would be to begin a practice of meditation. This is hard to do if you have never practiced quieting the mind, or really focusing on breathing. But start somewhere. Even if it is just for 2 minutes. Use headphones. Do it in nature. Do it in the bathroom or shower. Whatever you need to do, find a space, make the room, and make it a priority. Find some guided meditations on your phone, download an app. Once you start the practice, it gets easier. I promise. I only started with 2 to 3 minutes because I was unable to sit much longer than this without being distracted. I built up to 5 minutes, and then 10, and before I knew it, I was wanting to meditate for an hour. I remember the first time I spent a Sunday morning meditating for almost 2 hours. I felt so peaceful after, and from that moment I was addicted. Most would say this is time wasted, and I could have spent it doing something else. But it is a part of the programmed mind to think of it as time wasted. The spirit has no trouble with time. It is our ego that is in a constant state of rush. If we are truly serious about healing, then we will make time to help our minds heal. Once we understand how important it is to make time for our healing, and keeping our mind and body centered and grounded, we will not let anything stop us from making that a part of our daily routine, just like many make working out a part of it, or watching TV, or having their coffee in the morning. You will pick what is important to you.

I know many will begin this process because they are ready. They are ready to do that hard work. It is almost as if they look in the mirror one day and decide it's time. I can't tell you how to get to that point. Each of us find our own personal way. I think it does require some form of pain or discomfort, because without it, we may never desire to get out of the line. The line we are in is comfortable and familiar. Taking steps to see things outside of the line, see yourself differently, and change your perspective of the world feels risky and isn't easy. It is especially hard when you are in the line. Because when you are in the line, all you see is the line and everything outside of it seems wrong, or foreign— whether it is because you want to be in the line or because you were forced to be, or you may not even know you are in a line.

My encouragement is to take a step back and look at your life and all the choices you have made up until this point. Were they choices you made because you wanted to make them, or were they choices you made because someone else led you to make them? Do you believe in something because someone told you it is the only correct way to believe? Or did you explore the world and come to believe what you believe because of your own personal experiences, knowing within your own heart that you have found your way to what you know to be true. If you don't believe in anything, why do you not? What caused you to not believe?

After you stop and consider your life this way, take the time to go inward with what you came up with. Quiet the mind. Be mindful about how you want to move forward with these beliefs or non-beliefs. Is this thinking helping your life, and something you want to continue to do, or do you want to change something?

What is beautiful about life is that we can change it. It is hard to see that when we are in the line and all we are thinking about is what is in front of us or behind us. Trauma also keeps our minds in bondage and stuck believing we cannot change. While in the line we may see someone flying past us, and it might stir up some kind of reaction in us. I want you to think about what your reaction would be if you saw someone go by you while you were in line? Would you become irritated and angry? Or, maybe, you see the person pass, and you get curious. You start to think, I wonder what they see up there? Did they make it? Where are they going? Aren't they scared? How did they get brave enough to leave this line? Maybe you would slowly creep your head out of the line to look around?

Leaving the line is scary, but then, you take one small step out. You feel eyes on you, and you want to step back in the line for fear of judgment. You know that once you fully get out of the line, everyone in the line is going to be watching you, maybe even judging you, or possibly saying something negative about you. You think that leaving those people will leave you vulnerable and alone. This is where you have been and belonged for so long that you don't know what is outside of it. It looks a bit lonely out there, maybe even a bit daunting, but it also looks so freeing!

What if you never leave this line? What if what is outside of the line isn't what you think, but then again, what if it is amazing and you're missing out? What if you slowly start the drive, or the walk, or lay back and rest in the stream, and your leaf begins to float. What if!?

This is the most scary process. The beginning stages of change. It's like jumping off a cliff and not knowing what is on the bottom in the water below, hoping there isn't a scary fish or snake that will bite you, or a rock you may land on. But the thought of leaping off the cliff, the jump, it seems so liberating! You see other people doing it and you want to do it too. You look back and see the people not doing it, and you see their fear and why they aren't going for it. You understand both sides. But something in you keeps saying to jump! So, one day, you get all your courage up, and you just run! You run to the edge of the cliff and you jump off and fly through the air, feeling the wind, the gravity taking you down, and the freedom! The process of finally letting go, the fear, and the liberty at the same time! As you fall, everyone who has jumped before you cheers! You smile, you cry, you cringe! All the feelings come pouring out at once, all that you always wanted to feel! You aren't sure how to embrace them all at once because they have never been able to come out before, you have always contained them within the line, but now you are free! This is your moment! Freedom!

Then, you hit the water. You go under. It feels so deep, dark and scary, it feels like you are under the water forever. As you go under, the current takes you farther down than you anticipated and you start waving your hands and feet to get back to the top. As you do, you realize how tired you are, as if layers of your body are being shed in the process of trying to get back to the top. You have a sensation of having been swallowed up in a cocoon as if you were a caterpillar about to become a butterfly. It seems forever but slowly you start getting back to the top. You open your eyes and see a glimmer of light, and there it is, your first breath of fresh air after jumping. Your face hits the surface and you bounce your body out of the water and you smile. You did it! You are free! You lay there in exhaustion. Not just from the swim back up, but from the amount of energy it took to jump. To even get to the jump it took so much from you. But you did it! You broke through that fear, and now you are at the bottom of that cliff with all the others who jumped before you.

But as you look around, you might notice how quiet it is. There don't seem to be as many there like you anticipated. The line you left has more people, and you expected the same down here. Surely there would be more people who had jumped like you. Why didn't they jump? It was so freeing? But then you remember how hard it was. How getting out of the line was the hardest moment of your life, you knew that your old friends would begin to see you differently, and in that moment, you panic. What do I do now? You look back up the cliff you just jumped off of and realize there is no going back. You left the line, jumped through the fears, you experienced liberation and change, and it's a transformation you can never go back from. It's a freedom you can't un-experience. It's a freedom you feel compelled to speak about, and you want everyone to know what it felt like. Your awakening has happened.

This my friends, is what it is like to step out of the line. It is liberating and hard at the same time. I remember when I had my experience in 2016, I had a Christian song come to my mind with the lyrics, "walk in your freedom, walk in your liberty." I remember thinking, why in the world am I thinking of this song? So I began to do a study of freedom and liberty. I started to understand that freedom and liberty meant letting go, it meant being free of all the obstacles holding you back, breaking chains and moving forward without fear. The actual definition of liberty is the state of being free within society from oppressive restrictions imposed by authority on one's way of life, behavior, or political views. If you think about that, it means being completely free of anyone's power or control over you. This means that you allow yourself to be yourself without fear of what others believe or think of you. This is scary in a world where that seems to be all we focus on sometimes. We humans follow each other without even realizing it.

I want to point something out as I am talking about getting out of the line. I know I focused on my own journey of letting go of religion in this book, but I want to share that this line can be anything. It can refer to you needing to make a change of any kind. I want you to know that this can mean setting boundaries with people in your life that are hard to set boundaries with. It can mean deciding to give up a habit you have formed in order to self soothe, such as over-eating, drinking too much, or going out with friends you know are not helping you progress in life. These are all hard things to do. Especially when fear comes in, and your ego steps in telling you that you cannot survive without them. This is why it is so important to learn to love yourself first. It can be leaving a job that you know is sucking the life out of you and you are not showing up for your family at home in a loving way. The line you are in doesn't have to be religion. It can be anything that is holding you back from living your true authentic calling in life. Anything that holds you back from healing. But remember, you must first love yourself. Without loving yourself you are unable to fully heal anything in your life. You may be able to put a band-aid on it for a while and show up in what you feel is a good way for a while. But it will not be sustainable. Eventually, you will either go back to that thing that filled you, the line that you felt comfortable in, or find another line to become a part of, or something else that fills you up that can cover up your wounds and distract you from feelings, traumas, or stuck energy that needs to be healed.

You cannot fully understand what true healing is until you dive into your feelings of pain, fully embrace them, learn to know what they are, and love them. Yes. Love them. Love heals everything. In many of the meditations I did, I came to understand that in order to heal something, even pain or sickness, I had to send love to it. I would actually sit and meditate and tell the sickness and traumas in my body, "I love you, thank you for coming and serving your purpose in my body, but I no longer need you to be here, so you can go now." I then would invite the other parts of my healthy energy to go into that part of my body that was sick and merge them together in love. I did not always heal immediately, but to my surprise, I would almost always start to feel better about halfway through that day. I often think about what my dad said to me when he came to me in the dream. "Love is all that matters." It is such a powerful message. It really is all that matters. Truly, if that is all that matters, then love can be used for anything, even healing our bodies. So why not use love for healing trauma?

One of my favorite parts about my journey has been learning the process of healing and the importance of love. But also the importance of being around people who have that same loving energy you are wanting to become. Sadly, in the process of healing, you sometimes have to disconnect from others. This can mean family, friends, and it may seem as if you are often alone. I will say that my healing journey had many lonely moments. For a while I did not understand this. I felt as if everyone was leaving me at once. It wasn't something I had not experienced before, as I had struggled with relationships and friendships most my life because of my trauma, but something seemed to be triggering it even more so during my healing journey. However, slowly I began to notice something about myself. I was becoming more and more independent and learning boundaries. I am not suggesting you cut people out of your life during your healing process if you have positive people in your life. Keep as many positive, uplifting people around you as possible. But if you do not, and feel you need to disconnect, don't be afraid to do so. If you want to keep people in your life, set a boundary. If you need help, ask for help doing it. This is important in being able to find your own identity. Don't be afraid to learn who you are outside of these relationships.

I remember before this time I would watch others go on vacations or do fun things and be so jealous of their time. I always wished I had someone to do something with. Then one day it dawned on me. I do! I have me! It was then that I began to hang out with myself—and actually enjoy it. Not in a poor me, victim way, but in a freedom way. I began to take vacations by myself, go hiking alone, and find places I could spend time with myself. It was so freeing to spend time alone traveling. It was as if I was learning who I was, getting to know myself. I booked experiences where I would meet people and hang out with strangers and get to know them. I pushed myself out of my comfort zones so I would learn how to break out of my fears. I would take on some of the harder hikes just so I could challenge myself and go beyond what I thought were my limitations. I clearly remember a moment when I was hiking on a mountain and thinking about how amazing I felt. How free I felt. How I loved my own company and felt free of fear or worry. I remember so many friends saying things about how I inspired them, how brave I was, how they could never do that. I knew exactly what they meant; I had once thought that same thing. But I felt empowered! I was happy to inspire, but it was not my reason for doing so. As I began to do more and more of these things, I began to realize that I was my own worst enemy. I was the only one that held myself back from experiencing life. That life was meant to be lived and if I wanted to explore the world and live life, then I was the only one keeping myself from doing it. This body one day is going to cease to exist, and I don't want to waste the time I have in it any longer being trapped in a trauma mindset. I was going to find myself, heal, and live.

What is your reality? What is your dream? What is holding you back? Those are my questions. I know what it is like to worry about what people will think of you. I know people judged me in my healing journey. I know what it is like to worry about how you will feel when you lose a certain friend or have to set your first boundaries with someone you love so you can fully heal. It is a hard process. It takes work, and it takes help sometimes. Going to a therapist is not something to be ashamed of, and it was what I needed. Maybe you do too. Find someone you trust. Someone who will believe in you and see you. It may take a while to get to that person, but don't give up. Even if you make progress with one for years, if you suddenly find that you are no longer making progress, it is okay to decide to change. Being loyal to someone doesn't mean you have to forget about yourself.

Don't pick another human over yourself, especially your own healing. This was something I had to learn in my process. Had I never chosen myself, I would never have changed therapists. But I knew I was stuck. I knew I wanted to heal. I encourage you to evaluate where you are. If you are growing where you are, stay! Don't change. Maybe even have a real conversation with your therapist about your progress if you trust them. Tell them what you need and want. If they really are the right fit for you, and are there to help you heal, they will be all for hearing this! Most therapists want you to grow just as much as you want to. They want to sit in the dirt with you and hear your stories. If you find yourself with a therapist that doesn't seem to be as invested in your growth as you, please feel free to find another one. It is nothing against that particular therapist, it just means it is not a good fit.

Let me tell you the most powerful thing you will likely learn from this book outside of learning to love yourself. Silence does not protect you; it traps you. Read that again. The hardest part of my journey was learning to talk, to break out of my silence. Without breaking the silence of my story I would not have been able to start my healing journey. Silence is a trap that we build that somehow tricks our minds into believing it protects us. From silence we build our defenses. These defenses look like anything from addictions to control, hiding our feelings, emotions, our voices, and all of it keeps us hidden not just from others, but ourselves. This is where our own bodies began to work against us. We become sick, not just mentally but physically. We somehow believe holding on to our story allows us to remain protected or even protect others. But our silence perpetuates the process of slowly harming ourselves all over again.

Because I had believed that opening my scars would hurt more than the healing, I feared my voice for a long time. I feared sharing most of my story out loud, most of the story you just read in these pages. I feared even telling my therapist about it. It was in building that trust with her, opening up, using my own voice, that finally I began to taste freedom. I can't tell you it was easy. I often felt exposed and vulnerable, even physically ill at times because I had trained my body to not speak for so many years. The freeze response in trauma victims, especially those of sexual abuse and assault, is real. This is something I encourage you to give yourself grace in if you at all are experiencing it.

I had a hard time understanding my responses at first, but as I began to understand why I was freezing up this way I began to realize that it was a natural reaction to the traumas I had been through. Opening up and breaking your silence is freeing. It was by allowing my heart to become tender that I realized how much pain I had inside, how much anger. The more I spoke about, the more evident it became that I had so many things piled on top of one another inside my body that it physically had to be released, not just through my voice, but also through my body. There were times it would take days after therapy sessions for my body to become regulated again. After I began to understand that it was a part of the healing, and that my body was also having to get rid of the toxins of trauma I held in, I began to allow the process, to be patient with and kind to myself. I knew that if the energy didn't come out it would likely come out in another negative way. There would be times I would have to choose to take care of myself, setting boundaries to do self-care, and this was also new for me, but important, because it also taught me self-respect and love. I would have to learn to communicate clearly with others who remained in my life, even if they lived far away. When I was needing to work through something I needed to communicate that clearly so they had an understanding of what was happening in the moment. If I got into a conversation that was triggering to me and I felt cues in my body come up, I had to actually be honest about that with people instead of hiding the fact that I was feeling reactions in my body. I had to use my voice, not just in therapy, but in relationships outside of therapy. This was something I had never done before. This is why it is so important to have safe, trusting relationships during your healing journey.

Because I had spent so much of my life shutting my mind off to things in the past, I used things to protect myself such as alcohol or food. Eventually it became clear that those things where keeping me from progressing in my healing and that I needed to give them up and then start to heal without them. This meant having to finally feel things on a deeper level, learning how to tolerate that level of intensity, and opening myself to the process of letting my entire body feel it—not just a part of it. To let myself weep for the things I missed out on in childhood, or things I missed even in adulthood because I was protecting myself and wouldn't allow my layers of shields to come down to trust authentic moments with people. Because silence kept me shielded behind shame and guilt, I had pushed people away or hung on to them too tightly. Friends, if you don't hear anything else in this book, hear this. Shame will keep you silent, and silence doesn't protect you, and I promise you it will come out in another way. The most powerful thing I've learned from my amazing therapist is that shame is a lie, and you, I, we, can choose to no longer walk in it. But to no longer walk in it, we must expose it. Exposing it means getting it out of our bodies. Finding it, knowing where it comes from, experiences, feelings, and all. Be in your body, and let it happen. Break your silence. Find your safe person and place. Get quiet and meditate, breathe, and love yourself.

It wasn't until I was 38 that I started back in therapy full time, when I finally came to the realization of how much trauma I had not healed from. I tried many therapists in several years until I found an older woman who I felt I connected with and was able to work with for a few years. I did feel as if I made progress with her. However, due to religious reasons, my awakening process became more evident and we seemed to clash in many things regarding this. I did not feel this was a good fit after our views on religion began to diverge. That set me on the search for another which led me to my current one. As you can see, I went through several until I found one that fit my needs. So do not feel discouraged if it takes time. Healing is your own personal journey, and you must choose for yourself during it. For a long time I didn't realize this and would just go with what others wanted for me. I didn't realize how much choosing myself mattered until I finally started doing it. I knew I needed to be 100% honest about my traumas in my life and I knew I wanted a safe place to do this. I was determined to find a place and person I could do this with and until then I was not going to stop. At times, I still have the urge to run, but I know it is because of my trauma mind and breaking the silence and my ego wants to keep me stuck. But I no longer wanted to just brush up against my truth and not really dig into it.

I share this to encourage you in your healing journey to seek support you feel safe with. Someone with whom it is safe enough to expose the darkness, and break the silence. Remember, light always overcomes darkness. Finding a safe place doesn't mean it makes it easier, it just means it creates an atmosphere of healing, a place where you are challenged to be your authentic self. You need to feel comfortable enough to really dig into your traumas. Don't be afraid of the pain. Healing is not going to feel good all the time.

Love yourself! Be kind to your mind! Rewiring the mind takes time! It is most important you allow yourself to work through the process of healing and not rush it. I remember that I wanted to rush, to be better, to show up better, to show other people I was healed. I wanted to be healed, not necessarily for myself, but for others. When I finally learned to relax and allow the process to happen, I really started to heal. I wasn't healing for anyone but myself, and I needed to stop believing that I was doing it for others. Healing is about you, not others. Without loving yourself first, healing is just surface level.

Learn to say no! Once I started learned to say no, and that choosing myself was okay, I finally saw that the world would keep spinning without me. I found that my reactions didn't always have to be about what others wanted, and I didn't have to immediately jump to do what someone else wanted me to do, or what I thought they wanted me to do, because of fear of rejection. Doing things out of a fear of rejection meant I was denying myself the ability to have space to heal. Without the space to heal, the quiet, the room to say no and choose me, I constantly was choosing others, and this did not allow me space to heal.

Let yourself feel! Get angry, get sad, cry! I hit my pillow in anger, I yelled, I talked to myself in the mirror, I wrote things on paper and hung them around my house reminding myself to keep hope and be kind to myself. I spent time in nature hugging trees because I just needed a hug. I became friends with rocks because at times it seemed like they were the only ones that would get me. I don't know what your choice of getting the feelings out will be, or opening up your throat chakra to begin to speak of your story, but whatever you need to do, do it. Even if it seems silly. Trust me, trees are really good huggers, and rocks are good listeners when you need them.

Another thing I would encourage you to do is spend some time expanding your worldview. Not everyone has the resources or opportunity to travel as I have been able to, but if you get a chance, do it. Don't be afraid. You can even find somewhere close by, just across town to a different area that you don't normally go to, or a grocery store that you normally wouldn't shop at. And books are a fantastic resource too—you can look up what books are on the best seller lists or ask friends for some good stories about people different from you, who live in different cultures, or who go through different situations than you have—and they are free from a library near you.

I also understand that some of you may come from areas of crime, have low access to nature or natural remedies, or even a therapist. Maybe some of the things I have suggested in this book seem inaccessible to you. If this is the case, ask the universe, ask God, ask your higher power for a mentor, someone to come into your life and help you. I fully believe

that if you manifest something it will come to you. Believe you are worth it. Maybe you are the one that is to rise up in your area and be this person for the others. Maybe you're the one being called. Don't keep yourself small because someone once told you to stay small, or because you developed the belief about yourself that you will never reach another place than where you are now. I believe anyone can get to another place in life. There are many stories of this happening in the world. It is hard, yes. But take advantage of your own personal gifts. If you are an artist, paint, sell your paintings. If you are a photographer, take pictures. If you are a writer, write a book. If you are good at writing poems, write them. If you can read really well, read to someone. If you know how to grow plants, start a community garden or just a small one on your porch. Look for opportunities. If you don't know where to find them, ask! Know that you really do have the power in you to find your path in life. I fully believe this! I also believe that some of you may be the exact people that others are looking for on their healing journey. You are the resource! What is your heart telling you? Just look outside of what you know, your small world, the box your mind has been built in, and expand your thinking.

Have you ever seen the picture where there is a line waiting to get to Heaven? Here it is in case you haven't.

The Wait

author unknown

I remember seeing this when I was a Christian and thinking it was such a beautiful picture. I often thought, wow, how amazing, standing in line waiting for your turn to go to Heaven. All the people before you go, and then it is your turn. Something in me switched when I had my awakening in 2016. I suddenly realized that this is the line I don't want to be in. I don't want to just stand there, trying to do everything right to get to Heaven. I don't want to be molded and formed into something I am not, or to be a part of a line that has nothing to do with what my spirit originally was made to be when it decided to come and experience this human life. I want to live the life of my soul purpose, to be the energy of love on this earth, and I believe that means living a life outside of that line. Not to be a part of that line and waiting. Not conforming to what the programmed mind tells me to do, and keeps me believing. Or doing something just because my parents or grandparents believed or were taught to do it or believe it.

231

I believe that the line helped me understand what it is to be in it as well as outside of it. Without my knowledge of the line, I would have no idea what it means to be outside of the line. I would not be writing this book, and I doubt I would have gone through the healing I have gone through. I also doubt I would have come to the divine understanding that I have now of the true God energy that we are all really formed from. In my meditations I have seen and heard things I never would have seen or heard had I been shut off from the spirit like I was when I was in religious thinking. I am thankful for both experiences. But I am even more thankful to be free.

As I said before, no one can force another out of the line—the line that many are in and don't even want to be in. One must decide for oneself. This is the healing that needs to happen as well. Finding a way to start to choose yourself is going to be scary. Saying no is going to be scary. Trusting your intuition when you feel a ping coming up in your heart or chest or mind and you feel like something is off, and you decide to actually listen to it instead of ignoring it, will be hard the first time. You may think that you're just making it up, it is all going to be hard, at first. But you must start. You must start to trust yourself, and this starts by loving yourself. To love ourselves means to begin the process of losing our egos.

This is the very opposite of what the world tells us. The world tells us to build ourselves up! Believe in yourself, beat your chest until you feel powerful! But that is the opposite of what the spirit wants. The spirit wants the ego to be humbled. The spirit wants to be more than the ego, and in order for that spirit to become more, the mind must be deconstructed, over and over, sometimes a million times. It is a never ending process. I know this sounds exhausting to do. But I will tell you, once you began to get to know your true higher self, you become addicted to knowing yourself in that state, you become so in love with your true self, you want to be with your spirit and your divine love energy all the time. You will actually make the time to get to that place and it just becomes natural. It becomes who you are.

If you really want to use the teachings of Jesus, this is exactly what He was teaching. Love your neighbor as you love yourself. First love yourself, then learn how to really love others. There is a lot of evidence in mindfulness and meditation. Going inward, getting to know your own feelings, getting to know your trauma, getting to know who you really are underneath all that thick skin you had to develop as you were growing—it is going to be scary, but it will be freeing. Breaking down the barriers of armor and allowing love in, not just from others, but from and for yourself, is the key to true healing.

I never realized that my over-explaining to people was a trauma response. Then I started to see it. I noticed how I showed up in different spaces with different people. There were some people I didn't have any problems with. I could just say no, and be done. With others, I always felt I had to give some long explanation about why I was making the choice I was making to make sure they were okay with me making the choice. When I finally understood that it was none of anyone's business why I was deciding to do what I was doing, I stopped explaining my choices. It was hard. Really hard. One thing I love about my healing process, and something my therapist has been teaching me, is learning how to take my power back. Something she has said to me many times is, "When you feel guilty, that means you are choosing yourself." In my old way of thinking, the unhealed trauma mind, I would have never thought that way. I would have seen this as selfish. But it is not. It is power. Self-power. It is okay to have self-power.

Never choosing myself first has been one of the obstacles I have had to overcome even in writing this book. Many times I have questioned sharing my story. I have had many moments when I had to sit down and meditate just to work through my old trauma mindset popping its head back up and telling me I shouldn't share my story, that I should keep it silent. I finally came to the realization in this process of writing that it is my story to tell. It is my life, and I can stand in my power and spirit. It is also my healing. Oftentimes when I was in religion, I would look to others to come and rescue me or to God to come and heal me; for a miracle to happen and just make things magically work out. It is true that no one is going to show up and rescue you. No one is going to do the healing for you. No one can force you into an awakening. When you are seeking the truth, you will find it. I also believe that what you seek, you will find. It often comes in the places you least expect it to come.

I think about the story in the bible where the man has been beaten alongside the road and lay there waiting for help. Many people passed him by and many of those were religious men. Finally a Samaritan man stopped to help him. Oftentimes in life we are like this man on the side of the road, waiting for help from the people who are likely to pass us by. We might appear too bruised or broken, or have traumas that don't line up with their beliefs, so it is easier for them to move to the other side of the road and ignore the need. The programmed mind has us looking at those who seem to have it all put together for help, maybe even those who appear to have all the understanding and answers. Yet sometimes our healing comes in the least expected way. Maybe it comes from the exact thing you would normally turn away from. In this place is where you find the exact person that possesses the abilities and skills to provide help in the healing you desire, the abilities to support your journey. This is where true love exists.

> *But he wanted to justify himself, so he asked Jesus, "And who is my neighbor?" In reply Jesus said: "A man was going down from Jerusalem to Jericho, when he was attacked by robbers. They stripped him of his clothes, beat him and went away, leaving him half dead. A priest happened to be going down the same road, and when he saw the man, he passed by on the other side. So too, a Levite, when he came to the place and saw him, passed by on the other side. But a Samaritan, as he traveled, came where the man was; and when he saw him, he took pity on him. He went to him and bandaged his*

wounds, pouring on oil and wine. Then he put the man on his own donkey, brought him to an inn and took care of him. The next day he took out two denarii and gave them to the innkeeper. 'Look after him,' he said, 'and when I return, I will reimburse you for any extra expense you may have.' Which of these three do you think was a neighbor to the man who fell into the hands of robbers?" The expert in the law replied, "The one who had mercy on him."

Jesus told him, "Go and do likewise."

I do not say that all those who follow religions are like this. But many people are taught to think much like this, to believe that one belief or behavior or culture is above another, and to turn away from people because of these differences, even fearing them sometimes. This happens all over the world. The human ego has created so much greed, hate, destruction, and selfishness in our human behaviors that we often forget to love one another. I think it all comes from trauma and ego. Because most people don't have any idea they are doing it, we are stuck in an endless cycle of blame. Always making it about another person. Religion becomes a blinder to keep us in the blame game. We don't even know it. Religion wants us to separate good from evil, create barriers between love and darkness, and separate people according to rules and regulations that have no relevance to our wellbeing and our relationship to divine love. We want to believe that there is dark energy out there controlling things and that if we get near it, we might become consumed or contaminated by it. Yet we forget it is the light that consumes and destroys the darkness.

In my own experience I had no idea that religion was keeping me trapped in my own negative thinking and trauma. I believed that it was what was going to release me from my past trauma and negative thinking. It was where I believed that I would find freedom. I had no idea that coming out of the dogmatic religious mindset was what was going to free me, that I would find my healing in deconstructing my ego and breaking free from the system; that looking outside of the box for help and learning to love myself outside of a line I had learned to walk in would be the one thing that would allow me to finally overcome the darkness. Leaving that box allowed me to find my voice, to learn, to know I don't have to explain myself any longer, to know I could be me, and fully me, without explanation to anyone.

My heart goes out to you all. I am proud of you for making it this far in the book and sticking with me. I can imagine there were some triggering points for you in this book, as I had some of my own as I wrote it. The healing process is not for the weak, in fact, anyone who chooses to go on a healing journey is brave. I want you to know that even if you take one small step, you are brave, you are worthy, and you are worth it. I believe in you. I trust that you will find your way, and that you will be able to jump into the pool of healing love. And if you choose to leave the line and find yourself looking around, know you are not alone. I don't know what line you may find yourself in. Mine was the religious line. Yours may be completely different from mine. Just trust your intuition. That small voice you hear is often right, you're not crazy, you really are hearing from your spirit, from your guides, and from the true Divine Loving energy. It is real. Don't gaslight yourself. You got this!

Namaste.

Leaf Lessons

Follow me on Instagram:

@leaf.lessons_healing

#leaflessons_healing

Follow me on Facebook:

Leaf Lessons @angieharrisleaflessonsauthor.

About the Author

Angie is a mental health provider who came to the understanding of how important it is to not just heal through mainstream mental health services, but also, spiritually.

As she worked through healing many traumas in my own life from sexual abuse, mental abuse, physical abuse, rape, and religious trauma, she realized deep down under all the pain was who she truly was. The authentic Angie who had been hidden behind all the shame and guilt that came with such experiences. Angie never realized that facing the pain was how I would find her until I dove in and did the work.

As Angie worked through her own spiritual awakening process and healing, reprograming her mind, digging into old traumas, and facing things she thought would be buried forever, she began to shed weight physically and mentally.

Angie is certified in many wholistic healing modalities, including Meditation & Mindfulness, Reiki Energy Healing, Sound Healing, Life Coaching, and Women Circle Leader. She uses intuitive energy reading, psychic giftings and mediumship in her healing practice to help connect you with your own energy, purpose, and intuition. She also has an extensive history of working in the mental health field for many years, having training in trauma-based practices. All skills she now brings to the healing practice provided for others.

She is passionate about healing and especially supporting others on their healing journeys. Remember to lay back and rest in the steam of life and allow the flow to take you on your journey of healing and enlightenment.

References:

The Bible

What is the eightfold Path – Buddhism for Beginners

https://tricycle.org/beginners/buddhism/eightfold-path/)

Photo: The Wait – unable to find creator of this beautiful photo

Leaf Lessons

Made in the USA
Monee, IL
15 September 2022

14022360R00144